# Mousehole Childhood

## 1928-1950

# *Lily Polgrean Grose*

First published 2008

LANDFALL PUBLICATIONS
Landfall, Penpol, Devoran, Truro, Cornwall TR3 6NR
Tel. 01872 862581

A CIP catalogue record for this book is obtainable
from the British Library.

ISBN 978-1-873443-52-1

Cover painting by the author

All the photos in this book have been taken from the author's
personal family albums.

Printed and bound by R Booth Ltd, The Praze, Penryn, Cornwall


ACKNOWLEDGEMENTS

To my husband, John, for his encouragement and computer
assistance; to Colin, my son and Vanessa, my daughter, for their
interest in my writing; to my brother, Rev. Derek Polgrean and his
wife, Kathleen, for prompting some of my memories.
Also to Bob Acton for his checking of the typescript
and preparation for printing

# CONTENTS

To my grandchildren
Becky, Jamie, Isabel, Toby and Laura

# I love Cornwall

When I think of Cornwall, I have mental visions of steep cliffs, the sea, glistening in summer and gently rolling over golden sand, kissing the base of rocks and cliffs. In winter the waves are hungry, roaring and tossing up spray during the storms. I see the soaring and swooping magnificent seagulls and lovely pink thrift. Then, I see the beautiful yellow gorse, the primroses, daffodils, bluebells, camellias and rhododendrons.

I think of fishing boats, yachts, and large ships seeking refuge from the gales or coming into the docks for repair. I see the lifeboats crewed by brave men. The beaches have granite or serpentine pebbles, mussel, winkle and limpet shells.

Inland, I see the moorlands with the standing stones, the Merry Maidens, the Ring and Thimble, the Men-an-Tol and the quoits and cromlechs.

I think of the special food, wonderful pasties, saffron cake, hevva cake or heavy cake as it is now known, cream – clotted, of course – and the feather-light splits; then the fish, especially mackerel, crabs and lobsters.

Artists, galleries and potteries are remembered with affection. Also the stark landscapes with the ruins of engine houses of the tin mines, now part of our national Heritage. There is so much history all around us.

People were friendly, loving and caring during my childhood: they were proud of their heritage. I remember them with fondness.

Cornwall is more than a county. It is a Duchy with its own Saint Piran, the patron saint of tinners, the black and white flag and national day on March 5th. There is even a stirring anthem, *Trelawny*.

*    *    *    *    *

In this book, on which I have been making notes for many years, I have wanted to show life in Cornwall from the 1930's and I have written about growing up in Mousehole until my marriage in 1950 and leaving the village.

I hope you find my book interesting and enjoyable.

# My beginnings

I was born in London on 30th May 1928 in the New Cross area within the sound of Bow bells. My very Cornish parents teased me at times, saying that I was technically a Cockney, but I said, when I had understanding, that my parents had spoilt the pure Cornish line for me. I always tell people that I was born in London but am Cornish because I can trace my ancestors back to the 16th century.

Just as many Cornish drift back to their birthplace my parents finally went back 'home' when I was four years old, so my early memories of London are limited. Snippets are few. Indoors, I remember my high chair and an aspidistra in a large mauve and black decorated pot that stood on a high mahogany plant table. I remember a back garden with a trellised fence and a lamppost in the street near the front door. There was a police station nearby with a blue lamp outside.

*My mother and father at the time of their marriage*

My father grew up in Mousehole and both his parents were from families who had been involved in fishing in Mousehole for several generations. One of his ancestors, Richard Polgrean, had been a founder of Methodism in the village. Father did not follow the family tradition of fishing as, after leaving school, he learned the craft of 'tailoring' at Simpson's in Penzance. At the age of seventeen he joined the Army towards the end of the First World War, and served in Ireland and Germany. Afterwards he lived and worked in Northern Ireland for a while. In London he worked in Barkers, a large London store, as a display manager.

My mother lived in Mousehole until her marriage. Her mother also came from an old Mousehole fishing family, but her father, George Eddy, had been a stonemason in the Lamorna granite quarries before spending some years in quarrying in South Africa at the turn of the century. Whenever we went through Newlyn, Mother would point out the stonework and lettering on the Newlyn Art Gallery, which she said her father had done. Mother's three brothers, Wilfred, Gerald and Ronald, all emigrated to America in the 1920's, but not before Ronnie had been the goalkeeper in Mousehole's football team. They settled in Pennsylvania and only two of them returned for a brief holiday. Grandma Eddy visited them in America, bravely going on the journeys alone, as Grandpa Eddy stayed in Mousehole. My mother worked at West End Stores in Penzance, which was a drapery store. Her needlework and embroidery were excellent and much admired. When she married and was living in London, my mother,

*My christening with Auntie Rene as godmother*

at times, had a lodger living in our house. One was a lady (I don't remember there being a man) and her daughter Joan. Joan was of my age and we became friends and had many outings and picnics at Hilly Fields. However Joan developed a habit of biting me, and this became so bad that my mother had reluctantly to ask her lodger to find other accommodation.

My Christmas memories of London days are of family parties and going to the pantomime. It was *Cinderella* and I seem to remember the ugly sisters with vividly made-up faces mostly, possibly, because they frightened me. I remember telling everyone that I was Cinderella for many weeks after the pantomime, until my visiting aunts told me that, if I were Cinderella, then I did not live there and must go to the ugly sisters. My fantasies stopped at that.

Uncle Will, my father's half-brother, had followed his father as a fisherman, but his boat was sunk in a collision and one of the crew was drowned. He resolved never to go to sea again and moved to London with his wife Irene. He worked for the River Police and I thought of him as a very big policeman. Phyllis (four years older than me) and Harry (older again) were his children. Phyllis was a Brownie and I admired her and the uniform of brown that she wore. Somehow, her long brown woollen stockings intrigued me. I wore white socks in comparison.

*Uncle Will, with Harry and Grandpa Polgrean, who died before I was born*

Auntie Rene Polgrean and Auntie Gladys Polgrean were my father's sisters. Auntie Rene did not marry. She worked in London for many years as a buyer in lingerie departments of large stores and visited us frequently. Auntie Gladys worked as a tailoress and trained in Simpson's of Penzance. She met her husband when he was on holiday in Mousehole. He was from Yorkshire and worked for British Railways as a clerk. They came to London to marry because their close relatives were there and we all attended the wedding. Auntie Rene was the chief bridesmaid and cousin Phyllis, my friend Joan and I were the smaller bridesmaids. This was a happy and exciting day for all of us.

I remember Grandma Eddy staying with us in London. I was very close to her and she cared for me when my mother went into hospital for a thyroid operation. Grandma Eddy always styled her hair similarly to the style of Queen Alexandra and Queen

*The wedding of Auntie Gladys and Uncle Luther*

8

Mary. She loved toque hats and neat dresses – she was always a neat and tidy person but much smaller than my mother.

The story told to me many times was that one day Grandma, whom we called Mum as I had learnt to call her this because my mother called her Mum, was on her way with me to visit the hospital when there was a violent thunderstorm. Grandma Eddy had no umbrella and as she was passing a large house she saw a servant girl running up the steps of the house. She called to her and asked if she could shelter from the storm. When the storm eased a little, the maid suggested Grandma leave me with her, saying she would look after me until she returned from hospital to fetch me again.

When Grandma told my mother that she had left me in the charge of an unknown person, mother had hysterics and Grandma was sent to get me forthwith and bring me to mother to show her that I was alive. Apparently I was very happy playing with the kindly maid who had to give Grandma a cup of tea so that she could retrace her steps back to the hospital. I can remember seeing my distraught mother in a hospital bed. I had the impression of lots of beds and very white sheets everywhere with a few red blankets on some of the beds. I was frightened by hospitals for many years.

We moved to Brockley from New Cross before we left London to live in Mousehole.

*Lily with Grandma Eddy*
*(née Lily Trewavas)*

9

# Move to Cornwall

Our reason for leaving London was that my mother was heavily pregnant and my father was ill after having a mastoid operation. Possibly Grandma Eddy arranged for mother and myself to go to Mousehole; she may even have come up to London to fetch us. The home in Brockley was abandoned. Mother had

*Arrival from London at the "top" house for my first visit to Mousehole*

borrowed money from her parents to put a deposit on the house and the money was lost. However, father recovered from his serious illness and joined us. I was four years of age at this time.

We had visited Mousehole for holidays and I remember we stayed with Grandma and

Grandpa in the 'top' house as we called it. This was the first house in the row of four built by Grandfather and, later on, was the first one to be sold. Our family was given the cottage adjoining the top house to live in. This was the last of the four Grandma lived in later on in life, and I have described it separately as it had vivid memories for me. Grandma and Grandpa's second move was to 'Rosedene', the bottom house in the row, and this was my favourite house. It had four bedrooms, bathroom and toilet, a hall, front sitting room, back dining room and a kitchen and utility porch. There was a large outside washhouse too. I slept in this house often and can remember being concerned one Christmas that Father Christmas would not find me. He did! I can even remember my favourite present, a big doll with bisquit head and hands and a soft body.

*Lily, standing on the chair carved from granite by Grandpa Eddy*

10

Grandma and Grandpa's third move was into the next cottage which was called 'Island View' at the time. 'Rosedene' was put up for sale. I can remember their shock when the house was requisitioned (wartime rules). But it was sold for a much lower amount than it was worth. 'Island View', at the time Grandma and Grandpa lived there, had two bedrooms facing Mount's Bay and St. Clement's Island, and a back bedroom with a sloping roof. I could just stand upright at the highest point where there was a bed and large chest-of-drawers.

It was when I was sleeping in Grandpa's loft bedroom that the spiders came. I awoke one morning to see a family of large black spiders coming in from outside the small two-foot window at the foot of my bed. Just like Miss Muffet, I screamed and jumped out of bed heading for the door to escape, still screaming of course! I reached the large chest-of-drawers when Grandpa appeared in the doorway wanting to know the reason for my panic. Shaking, I pointed at the intruders. However, Grandpa just smiled and told me to stop screaming and not to be so silly. I probably screamed all the more loudly and Grandpa, annoyed at having been awakened so early, told me that if I did not stop screaming, he would make me stop by putting the spiders in my mouth. So much for child psychology! I just kept on screaming and mother arrived from next door. I told her what had happened and she comforted me and took me back home. It was the last time I slept in the loft in the condition it was then. But from then on I developed a great horror and fear of large spiders – especially the harvest ones which come into our houses in Cornwall in September and October.

Of course, Grandpa was a kindly but strict person who really loved us deeply. He used graphic language and didn't understand how sensitive children could be. We lived in the two-bedroomed 'Island View' until the grandparents thoughtfully realised that my brother Derek and I were growing up and that we all needed more space, which meant that I did not have to sleep in their house. They decided to swop cottages, including the house names. This was Grandma and Grandpa's fourth move.

So, 'The Queach' became the lower cottage and 'Island View' the top one. Our brass name plate went with us and was proudly screwed on to the outside porch. At this time, I remember our water closet was across the yard opposite the kitchen window. Derek slept in the loft, and I had the front single room. After Gran Polgrean died, father had some money left to him from the sale of her house. So the cottage received a face lift. We took in the loft which was above the next door (Grandma's) washhouse and heightened the loft walls. A wonderful bathroom with toilet was created and a double-sized back bedroom. The downstairs bumpy kitchen walls were made smooth and, after dealing with all the particles of stone and the dust, we were all happy. A piano now had pride of place in the front room and I commenced lessons.

All our friends and many relations came to admire our pretty pink bathroom, as ours was one of the first of such luxuries at that time. We had hot water when we switched on the immersion heater in the airing cupboard in the new back bedroom. Of course, we still had the outdoor water closet, too.

# Grandma Eddy's Cottage

*The Kitchen*

Most kitchens in Mousehole were similar to the one belonging to my Grandma Eddy, née Trewavas; however certain objects personalized this kitchen cum livingroom. A gramophone was an exciting object – I was allowed to use this under supervision. There were several records of hymn singing and happy tunes such as 'The sun has got his hat on'.

When my cousin Phyllis was visiting Mousehole from London she was allowed to bring her latest records to Grandma Eddy because her Grandma had no record player. Unfortunately one day she put one of her records on the armchair by the radiogram whilst she lifted the heavy oak lid of the player and I, who was four years younger than her, accidentally knelt on it. Of course it broke and she burst into tears. I have never forgotten that carelessness on my part!

A very big round mahogany table dominated this room. It had claw feet and our feet either knocked against them or we had to rest our feet on top of the claws. There was always a cloth on the table, and for mealtimes the thick day cloth was replaced by a spotless white linen one. There was a chiffonier containing the best china. It had a large carved top which touched the wooden beams of the ceiling. A large oil lamp stood on the shelf in case the electricity failed, which it did during gales and storms when the overhead lines were blown down.

Across the room on the wall was a small cupboard by the black leaded range. The cupboard housed the daily used crockery and cutlery. The bottom part was used for cooking utensils. The black leaded range was called the 'slab'. The fire inside the slab provided warmth and heat for its oven. The slab was trimmed with brass and was cleaned until it shone brightly. The black slab was cleaned with a black lead polish. The cooking from the oven was delicious but there could be disasters with cakes because exact temperatures were difficult to maintain. Special cakes such as Christmas cakes went down to the village bakehouse. Grandma's kitchen walls were covered with family photos, and there were animal heads complete with horns. The larger one was an Ankole and the smaller, hanging at the top of the stairs, was a Springbok. I do not think Grandpa shot the animals himself, but he brought them back from South Africa.

*Grandma Eddy outside her cottage*

I liked the blue glass rolling pin, which hung above the window. There was also a green fishing float covered in netting on the curtain pole. There was a glass barometer which foretold the weather; there was a glass insect trapping device – what a lot of glass objects the Victorians used! In the summer fly papers were used to trap wasps and flies. These yellow sticky papers hung from the curtain pole. I did not like seeing struggling insects on the papers, however being stung by a wasp was not an enjoyment. Grandma lived in the next cottage to us so it was easy for us to go into her kitchen which was more fascinating than ours.

From the back door a washhouse was reached by walking under a covered way which protected one from the elements. This was very necessary because the toilet was in a little boxed-in space in the corner of the washhouse. On Mondays the washing was done, and Grandma and my mother took all day doing this. There was a big stone sink with cold piped water. The water needed boiling in the big galvanized boiler; at least this was easier than when the water had to be fetched from half way down Raginnis Hill from the 'shoot', which supplied running water from a spring in the hills above it. In earlier days the water had to be carried in pails back up the hill to the cottages before the washing ritual began!

When the water was heated the washing could begin. The clothes were rubbed on a wooden dolly board and they were then rinsed in the stone sink. A blue dolly bag was whisked around in the water as an aid to whiten the 'whites'. Another process was starching when sheets, shirt collars and cuffs, blouses, tablecloths and aprons were dipped in a creamy solution which was obtained by using boiling water added to chalk-like lumps. The clothes were then put through the mangle – a giant pair of wooden rollers turned by a large handle. The mangled clothes were then folded and placed in the wicker basket, known as the flasket, ready for open-air drying. The flasket had to be carried to the garden up fifteen or so small steps. When dry the clothes were brought down to the cottage again and sheets and tablecloths were pulled straight by two people. I thought this was the only 'fun' part of washday.

Ironing was usually done the next day on the kitchen table in our cottage because Grandma's table was 'best' mahogany. The flat irons were heated on the slab and experience was needed to guess the correct heat. The old sheets, used as protective covering of our wooden deal table, showed many scorch marks. There was much joy when a few years later Mother had an electric iron and there was no need to guess the required heat from the flat irons!

*Grandma's Bedroom*

This room had a tiny fireplace the size of a basket. It had never been used, but above it there was a small mantelpiece which had many 'treasures', glass or brass objects arranged on its shelf. There was a bedside cupboard containing the chamber pot. On the top of the cupboard was a Bible. There was a huge chest of drawers on which beautiful chandeliers twinkled with rainbow lights and in a breeze the prisms sang with wood chime-like tunes.

The dressing-table was always covered in crochet mats and on them hand mirrors, brushes, pin trays and ring trees were arranged.

A stuffed owl sat wisely on a small shelf. Children did not have free access to the bedrooms.

In the second bedroom there was a wardrobe, a dressing table, a large chest of drawers and a washstand. A lovely china washbasin and jug, which I inherited, stood on the washstand. Of course, the jug had to be filled with cold water unless the water was heated on the slab downstairs in the kitchen. Washing was consequently a fairly quick affair.

After Grandpa died, I slept in this room for many months, as Grandma was nervous of being alone in the house at night.

*Granny's Parlour*

This was a sacred place, which housed the Family Bible and became a 'Chapel of Rest' on appropriate occasions. The Minister was always invited there for tea and biscuits. Privileged relatives entered the room for talks with Grandma and Grandpa.

This room had carpet on the floor and the curtained window area had a small window seat. Cold refreshment stood there. There was a three-piece suite, a big Maidenhair Fern, and a glass cupboard containing mainly books.

The fireplace was surrounded with a brass fender and a companion set, brass-handled cleaning tools, was inside the fender, and above the mantelshelf was a lovely bevelled edge mirror. Treasures on the shelf were large ornaments, a china cow, lustreware dishes and trinket boxes.

The wallpapered walls were covered with family photographs. One which attracted me was of a lovely child with long curly hair. She was wearing a dress trimmed with ribbons. I learned that her name was Lily, which was my Grandma's name and is also mine. Lily had died of diphtheria not long after the photo was taken. She had been Grandma's daughter and a sister of my mother who was called Rose.

There were framed engravings hanging on the wall above the settee and under each picture was a description in French. When I was courting, John was a frequent visitor to this parlour and as he was studying French he was intrigued by the pictures. Unfortunately the pictures were not handed down to us. There was also a framed photo of a very important-looking man and we were told that he was Charles Trewavas, Grandma's father. Another Charles Trewavas had been town clerk of Manchester.

# Grandpa Eddy

Grandpa spent hours collecting snails and slugs from his field on Raginnis Hill opposite our cottages. If the French crabbers came along his hedges with their sack collecting his snails he would shout at them and wave them away. Personally, I thought he would have been helped if he had let them loose to do their collecting amongst his vegetables. However, this was not his way of thinking. We loved his vegetables. Grandpa, of course, was not collecting the snails to eat. The French crabbers probably were.

I remember my Grandpa's kindness when he paid the postman's money so that I could have the Christmas present of a necklace sent to me by my American penpal. I could not pay the custom duty, neither could my father at this expensive time, so Grandpa came to my rescue.

Grandpa was a tall man and he had a bushy moustache. He had worked as a stone mason and was employed with the Lamorna Quarries. As the result of an accident, he had lost the tip of the index finger of his left hand.

His birthplace was a pleasant granite cottage in Lamorna Valley. His travels included South Africa where he had worked in stone quarries. When he returned to Cornwall, he built the two houses on either side of the existing cottages on Raginnis Hill where we lived.

He died in 1945, and I felt very sad. I shut myself in our outside toilet to shed my tears in private.

He was buried at Paul Cemetery.

17

# Gran Polgrean

Gran was my father's mother. She lived in the heart of the village, but her house did not have a view of the sea as she lived at Eden Place, fairly near Mill Pool. It was a nice granite house, but in the wrong place if you wanted a pretty view from your front windows.

Grandpa Polgrean was a fisherman and owned his own boat. I did not know him: he had died before I was born. There was a lovely cobbled entrance at the side of Gran's house leading to a little yard at the back of the house. On the left hand side of the yard was a building containing a kitchen and a loft, presumably for fishing nets in Grandpa's day. There was a nice toilet in the corner of the yard. Across the yard from the building was the back door of the main house.

Gran was a stern looking person but was always neatly dressed. She was pleasant to be with, but she had had a hard life. In addition to having my father and his two sisters she had inherited Grandpa's family as his first wife had died. Uncle Will and Auntie Phyllis were children of his first marriage, and there were several other children who had married and left the village. One of them had gone to Australia and settled there.

We went to see Gran occasionally and when Auntie Gladys was on holiday we had some lovely meals together. I particularly remember the tinned red salmon, which was served in a large lead crystal glass bowl, and wonderful salads.

Gran visited us at Raginnis Hill, had some meals with us and always wanted to do a job to help out. Mother usually had her clean the cutlery.

She had an illness when I was of Infant School age and my mother made meals for her. I carried the plates or soup basin covered in a tea towel to her on my way back to school after I had my dinner. One day I was teased by some boys on my way to her and Adam Torrie rescued me and escorted me to Gran's. He was a very nice man and looked out for me daily and carried the meal to Gran's for me. Adam Torrie had been on the SS *Baltic*, which was wrecked on St. Clement's Island. He stayed in Mousehole after his rescue and married a local girl. His boys went to Mousehole School and one of them, Marrack, was in my class.

Auntie Gladys looked after Gran after her illness. She fetched her and took her back to Pudsey in Yorkshire where she was living at the time. Gran's house was then sold.

I have a 'sampler' embroidered by Gran when she was ten years of age, It states 'Annie Matthews finished this work May 28 1872'. She was a marvellous needlewoman.

Gran died in 1940. I felt a great sense of loss even though she had been with Auntie Gladys and away from Mousehole for some time. I did not go to her funeral service at Mousehole Chapel - children rarely went to funerals in those days. I stayed for the day with Mrs. Osborne at 'Bryn-mor', a few houses down the hill from our cottage. Mrs. Osborne was a friend of our family and she tried to comfort me.

Gran Polgrean was buried in Paul Cemetery.

# Mousehole childhood

*Two family pictures of Mousehole about 1930:*
*(Top) Auntie Gladys at the head of the new quay with baskets of long lines*
*(Bottom) Auntie Rene and Auntie Gladys in front of the many boats which*
*fished from the harbour at that time*

We felt secure growing up in Mousehole. There were always local residents about: people were not nosey. They just kept a kindly lookout for fellow inhabitants and their children.

A river ran through Mousehole to the harbour where it poured out from the wall onto the rocks. We avoided this area, but I had to walk past the 'river', as we called it, on my way to and from school.

One day a girl from my infants' school class, Barbara, grabbed my precious possession, my stamp album, from me and threw it into the 'river'. It was fished out for me by one of the 'big' boys and I carried the

*Lily (aged 7) and Derek with our mother on the hill opposite 'Rosedene'*

sopping wet album home. No doubt I was in tears, as we spent most of our little pocket money buying stamps for our collections. Sixpence would buy a packet of about 4 stamps.

Barbara's parents, cousins of my mother, were told of her diabolical action and reprimanded her. Her mother made her apologise to me and allowed me to choose one of her stamps to add to my collection. I even remember which stamp it was because it was housed in a new album. I still have my collection. Barbara became my friend and we spent time drawing and playing together. We designed bikinis and skirts from the bladder wrack and sea lettuce seaweed on the rocks below the Salt Ponds. (These salt works proved uneconomical in the past and were soon abandoned.) Barbara and I are still interested in art.

Brenda Worth lived behind the Millpool area and she and I discovered the challenge of climbing up and down chain ladders. There were several of these around the harbour and when the tide was in small fishing boats were moored below them. We could even jump on to the decks of the boats as there was rarely a dangerous gap between the boat and the harbour wall. We enjoyed exploring the small cabins and imagined going out to sea. However, we never did go out on one of these boats. Eventually, the novelty of this new game wore off.

*My 8th birthday party at 'Rosedene'*
*(l. to r.) Front row: Mary Bailey, Dora Price, Vera Williams*
*Top row: Jean Brownfield, Lily Polgrean, Ada Williams, Brenda Worth*

*Lily and Derek in the Cove*

Rock climbing in the coves was great fun with whoever would be available to come along with me. The Hotel Rock in the first cove was our favourite place – it was our imaginary castle. Playing shops just needed a little imagination with plentiful seaweed, shells, pebbles and wild flowers from the cliffs behind the beach. We caught shrimps in the rock pools in our nets and then put them back in the pools again before we went home. We caught small fish (known to us as 'bullcats' or 'bods') in the pools with cotton and bent pins. Bait was a piece of limpet knocked off a rock. These, too, were released to their watery homes. Crabs were found under the rocks as the tide went out and examined carefully before being put back in their

22

*Catching bullcats*

hollows again. The boys made small boats out of pieces of cork washed up on the beach, with a small slate for the keel and a feather for the sail. These were 'carkers' and there were also 'kiskies', fashioned from the long leaf of a reed. The boys played cricket on the 'Por', which was the harbour when the tide was out. Usually the stumps were pieces of driftwood.

When I was very young I got stuck on the rocks by the Cave. A schoolfriend and myself had always been warned not to go down to the Cave and over difficult rocks alone, but one day we did go on this adventure alone. Our parents did not know where we were. I was younger and smaller than Aronwyn, and when climbing back from the lower rocks I could not get a grip on the iron bars embedded in the rocks to assist climbing. It was beginning to get dusk. In the end Aronwyn decided to go back along the narrow pathway to the main thoroughfare of Raginnis Hill. I worried about what could happen if she did not return. Gulls were eerily whirling and screaming overhead and I kept remembering that children had been swept off rocks by freak waves and had drowned. There had been many falls too. However, when I was almost in tears, Aronwyn came back with a strong lady I knew was Ruth Adams, an artist. She hauled me up to safety and we walked back again to the safety of the Hill. She was very kind and brushed away our thanks.

*Auntie Gladys at the Cave*

Playing 'houses' in the flower loft with Marie Giles in the yard at 'Asphodel' at the beginning of the 'Crackers' was great fun. (She recently called on us during a visit from New Zealand, where she is now living.)

There were still some vestiges of the fishing industry in the village when I was very young. Pilchards were still being pressed in some fish cellars and

23

women worked in them, placing the fish in large barrels and layering them with salt before they were placed under a heavy press. This industry soon died out and the work moved to Newlyn. In the early years of the century, there had been fish cellars all over the village and most of the village women were involved in this work during the pilchard season. A picturesque side of fishing could be seen when the fishermen 'barked' their nets in huge vats close to the harbour. This was a tanning process to preserve the nets and, after being taken from the vats, they were hung over the railings of the 'Cliff' and spread down over the wall to the harbour. The pungent smell of the drying nets is an abiding memory. Village folk always said, when they were offered a very dark cup of tea, that it was as 'strong as bark'.

Life was never dull or boring and we were happy. We took part in plays, singing, walking, swimming and skimming contests with the flat stones we used to skim over the flat water in the Cove.

Blackberries were gathered in season and when our legs were stung with nettles we found dock leaves, which with a little spittle eased the pain.

Our dolls were always christened (baptised) in the water from a little fern-veiled well which was in the right-hand hedge on the way up the hill to Raginnis just past the path to the 'Crackers', which was on the left.

*Learning to swim with cousin Phyllis; Auntie Phyllis in background*

I was taken to the large Whitsun Fair, held in Penzance, by my Grandmother Eddy. I was allowed to ride on the children's roundabout and Grandmother rolled some pennies to try to increase her initial penny to sixpence or even a shilling, but without success. Then we wandered to the sideshow area and saw outside a tent a placard inviting people to view the headless woman, a medical wonder. There was no queue outside, so Grandmother and I went inside the tent. There, inside a glass container, sat the headless woman. There were tubes coming out of a contraption on her neck and there was no sign of her head. I was fascinated! However, Grandmother quickly took me outside again. I remember this incident vividly. It must have been a trick, but how did the fair people contrive this apparition?

Famous artists came to Mousehole to live and work. They were respected by the locals and lived happily amongst them. A film company (Ealing Films) came to the village, which became a French fishing village for the film "The Foreman went to France", in 1942. Several local people acted as 'extras'. We eagerly clamoured for the stars' autographs, as autograph collecting was another of our hobbies. Myra Humphreys gave me a sheet of paper to collect mine, as Raginnis Hill was a quarter of a mile outside the village. I had famous names such as Constance Cummings, Tommy Trinder, Clifford Evans, Gordon Jackson (his first film), Robert Morley and Alfie Bass. Unfortunately,

during my various moves when married, my autograph book disappeared.

Myra and I were very good friends. We tried to learn dancing listening to Henry Hall on the radio in her parents' sitting room, followed by a light supper. We went to local events and fêtes together. Fancy dress competitions were part of the fun at the Tregenza's Garden Fête on the Parade. On one occasion I was a Japanese girl, complete with paper sunshade. Lucky dip or bran tub presents were popular.

Sylvia Pender was a good friend and I stayed with her in her parents' house when my father was ill with pneumonia. I loved being with them: they were a warm-hearted family. Sylvia and I had no difficulty in playing games together - we both had imagination. We made up stories with

*My fancy dress*

ourselves as the main characters. Sylvia had a John Bull printing set; this had rubber strips with the alphabet embossed on them. The little squares with the letters were cut out and then placed in a wooden holder to made words and messages. This was then inked by pressing onto an ink pad. Painstakingly we printed out messages and letters. Our favourite ones were invitations to a wedding or a party. These were addressed to famous people such as film stars. The invitations were never sent but we acted out the situations we imagined.

Most of my friends were members of the Ovaltineys' Club. I was an Ovaltiney and enjoyed being a member. We were Ovaltine drinkers and had badges, rule books and a secret code. It was exciting to be able to write messages in code to fellow Ovaltineys. We had our own song: "We are the Ovaltineys, little girls and boys..." There was a programme on Radio Luxembourg on Sunday afternoons and we listened to our Club news. Of course there was always a message for us in our code.

*Sunday School*

We attended Sunday School twice on Sundays in my childhood and our friendships there at St. Clements were well bonded. The Second World War was declared when I was eleven years old. I was attending worship in St. Clement's Methodist Church at the foot of Raginnis Hill. The Service had just begun and a steward climbed the pulpit steps and spoke to the Minister. This important news was then announced to the congregation.

Many of Mousehole's children's reading books were prizes for attendance at Sunday School. The higher the marks for attendance, the better the quality of the book awarded. The Secretary of the Sunday School went to the bookshop, Saundry's in Chapel Street, Penzance, and chose the books annually. There was also a Christmas tree, and toys or books were gathered under the tree and then distributed to all the pupils.

*The Old School Hall*

Before the Mousehole School I attended was built the children of the village attended a school in the large building opposite the new granite buildings. The large hall with a platform was used for concerts and plays in my childhood.

I took part in some of the plays and concerts and in particular can remember being Bo-Peep in a Nursery play. In this Old King Cole, played by Gavin, was supposed to speak to each character as they approached his throne. To me he should have asked, "What are you looking for, Bo-Peep?" and I would reply, "I have lost my sheep, sir". There should have been another line from the king, which I have now forgotten, and then I would have taken my place, with the other characters, by his throne. However, the King forgot me and went on to the next character coming on stage. I was left wandering about in limbo on the stage until I gave up waiting for my cue and went to my position by the throne.

I was devastated. My lovely blue and pink long dress was wasted on my non-speaking part. My lovely shepherdess' crook, especially made for me, seemed a waste. I remember the disappointment I felt. I felt even more unhappy for Uncle Tom Eddy who had fashioned the crook with great care.

I fared better as Little Miss Muffet another time and had a solo spot dancing the sailor's hornpipe the following year.

Friendships made during childhood have a lasting quality.

*Boats filling the harbour, about 1930*

# Mousehole schooldays

My first teacher at Mousehole School was Mrs. Legg who was a local lady. She was very kind and gentle, and an ideal person to teach children attending school for the first time. We had an infants' building which contained two classrooms and a cloakroom with rows of hooks placed at different heights. There were no indoor toilets at this time; they were across a gravel playground. We were encouraged to use these facilities only when dressed in warm coats at playtime during the winter months.

After being gently initiated to school life by Mrs. Legg, we moved up to Miss White's classroom where we were prepared to advance to the Junior school which was a completely separate building. Miss White's room was larger than Mrs. Legg's. There was space for a large blackboard and cupboards. We had room for drama – performing short plays. There was a large stuffed owl on one cupboard. Its large eyes seemed to watch us as we worked and played.

I was called forth every time we mimed 'Rumpelstiltskin' because I was the best performer who could fall elegantly to the floor when the Princess pricked her finger on the spinning wheel!

Miss White was very keen on teaching the girls sewing skills. I made several white cotton pillowcases by hand. Embroidery was taught by using cross stitch place mats and decorating bright blue pinafores with red and white simple stitches – crosses plus the equals sign. The boys did puzzles at this time or had games involving arithmetic.

The next teacher in the 'big' school was Miss Ethel Williams. Handwriting and compositions were my favourite subjects now, followed by art and geography. She encouraged public speaking by asking pupils who had had a special holiday to speak to the class. I enjoyed writing stories and at times was asked to read these to the class. Thankfully, they were well received.

We loved Empire Day when a very large map was draped over the blackboard and we each had a little pointer to point out on the map a little piece of the British Empire, as it was. I can still remember my piece, which was, "And all these little islands dotted around." As part of our local history, we were told about Dolly Pentreath, the Mousehole woman who was supposedly the last person to speak the Cornish language. She is commemorated by a monument in the wall of Paul Churchyard and a tablet on the cottage where she lived near the Keigwin Arms.

Another teacher was Miss Nellie Richards. I remember milk monitors being appointed at this time; they were older girls from the top classes taught by Mr Frank White and the Headmaster, Mr. Elford. We had a third of a pint of milk during playtime or Horlicks tablets. We had singing lessons and gas mask drill, and air-raid practice when we went into the large cloakroom and sat on the floor. The latest songs were sung to keep up our morale! We carried our gas masks with us everywhere we went during the war years.

Our wooden desks in the classrooms had inkwells built into them, and we used steel nib pens and our own fountain pens for writing.

The Headmaster's study also served as an inspection room for the nurse's health check, which included nit inspection. Luckily I was not troubled by an infestation of these parasites.

Gardening was popular but we had only little plots in the playground and our tools were forks or blunt kitchen knives.

Toilets were outside at the very top of the playground. Favourite games were rounders, deck tennis, hopscotch, quoits and skipping.

I remember our class from school went "beating the bounds" of the new boundary of the borough of Penzance which was enlarged to include Mousehole in 1934. This involved a hilly walk which took us to the new boundary stone situated in the hedge of the lane leading to 'The Crackers'. There, the Mayor, Alderman Birch, 'beat' the stone with a bunch of twigs and made a short speech.

When the evacuees came during the war years, they were from the East End of London. They were the Jewish Free School, and their teachers came with them. They were billeted in local homes and took over the whole of the Infants School, where they were taught. We mixed with these children in the village and especially when visiting the beach. They were mostly nice children and we compared their Jewish culture with our own Methodist upbringings. In particular, I remember one of the nice boys, whose name was David Sacs. One of the teachers' wives was expecting a baby at the time they lived in Mousehole. They often came to the beach at the Boys' Cove and I noticed that the husband was very solicitous towards his wife. He settled her on cushions by their favourite rock, which was a perfect shape for resting her back, and wrapped rugs around her against the sea breezes. I watched with great interest – it was so romantic!

The eleven-plus year was a disaster for the school. Although a goodly number excelled in the pre-exam intelligence test, no one passed the final eleven-plus exam. I know there were brilliant scholars in our group who finally excelled in their chosen professions. The Headmaster had an assembly in the playground to announce the results. The scholars who had taken the exam were all called to stand in line at the front of the assembled upper school and a distraught Head made the failed students feel very inadequate. I felt very disappointed because I wanted to learn new subjects in a new environment.

Several pupils went to Art School and, although I was chosen to apply for a Scholarship to Penzance Art School, my chosen career had been decided by attending some evening classes with Miss Wesley at Penzance Commercial College. Jean Brewer chose the same path and Miss Wesley accepted us as paying day students. Here, we studied shorthand, typewriting, arithmetic, bookkeeping, English, spelling, commercial correspondence and other subjects. Miss Drew, who taught us typewriting, gave us many awkward spellings, especially with double consonants. I always remember 'occasion' and 'accommodation', but 'vicissitude'? Would we ever need to spell that word correctly? Nevertheless it was good for us to look the meanings up in the dictionary. Miss Friggins, who taught us other spelling, gave us a good mnemonic for vicissitude – 'Remember, it has a 'ciss' in the middle', she said, and, being the romantic thinking teenagers we were, we did remember! However, for us the 'ciss' was a 'kiss'!

I took examinations in most of the subjects (RSA, Pitman's and the London Chamber of Commerce) and became equipped to work as a secretary in Penzance. This meant a 3-mile bus or cycle ride every weekday. Jean and I travelled together on the same bus. Waving to the lad who manned the weighbridge at Penlee Quarry lightened our journey. His day was brightened too, because he looked out for our bus and his waving became ever more lively! We never knew his name. Jean and I became good friends. We shared many outings and interests, played piano duets at village concerts and went for a holiday together to my Aunt Gladys' in Nottingham. We shared lots of giggles, too!

Later in life, I obtained further secretarial and teaching qualifications at Cornwall Technical College.

# Our Pets

*Dogs*

*Grandma Eddy's dog Nell*

Nell was a black mixed breed, half Pug. She was given to Grandma as she was the result of carelessness at the kennels, although her parents were high class thoroughbreds. She was a great friend of mine during my schooldays and I took her for walks frequently. Going out to the 'Crackers' was a favourite walk, although through the fields to the first Kemyel farm came second favourite. I kept her mostly on her leash. Sometimes a friend came with me for my walk.

One day Nell and I were going to the Crackers which led to the Coastguard lookout hut and the path was edged with fields blazing with wild daffodils in Spring or cultivated fields of anemones and violets. The views were fabulous, sea, rocks, cliffs and boats. I remember we had passed the stile leading to the Kemyel fields when Nell stopped, sniffing at something which slithered away into the hedge. She gave a little yelp and to my horror I guessed that she had been bitten by an adder. I realised that if it had happened a little later I could have been bitten in my foot or leg. I had to get Nell back home as quickly as possible and we ran all the way back to Grandma. Nell's face was very swollen when we got back. Grandma was very upset when she saw this but she called the neighbours who had a telephone and rang for a taxi. Mother and Grandma went to the Vet at Penzance. And luckily the treatment Nell received saved her life. She lived to a good old age and we went for many more walks.

31

*Our dogs (1) Skipper*

Skipper was a miniature Yorkshire terrier, very tiny and a lightweight after Grandma's Nell. He was not a lapdog and was not very affectionate, but he

*Skipper begging for wedding cake*

loved his walks. We had taught him to sit up and beg for titbits which he did very well. His favourite walk was the 'Crackers' and he was energetic, pulling at me urgently if I was walking slowly. However we all loved him and were very unhappy when he disappeared. On Bonfire Night we put Skipper in Grandma's kitchen with her. She too loved his company as her dog Nell had died of old age. The fireworks from the village were not too loud when our windows and doors were tightly closed. Unfortunately, someone knocked on Grandma's door, and, without thinking about Skipper, she opened it. At that moment a very loud bang sounded from nearby and that firework frightened Skipper who dashed past Grandma and ran dementedly up the hill. We were alerted and ran after him. We never found him and a week later one of the 'Crackers' field workers found the body lying near the cliffs. Poor Skipper. We all mourned his passing and have never forgotten the need to protect animals from the noise of fireworks.

*(2) Ching*

*St Clement's Island in background*

Ching was definitely my mother's dog. He adored her. She had total control of the long-haired, white and black Ching. He was friendly, plump and slow moving, but he loved his walks and I enjoyed taking him out when I stayed with mother. He loved his food and an occasional piece of chocolate or semi-sweet biscuit.

I had left Mousehole when my mother had Ching as I had married and moved to West Hartlepool. Ching was a

32

good companion to my mother who did not go out walking because of her arthritis. Ching remembered us and welcomed us when we returned to Mousehole for our annual holidays. He frequently sat close to me, often on my feet; he wanted me to stay at mother's to ensure he had his walks. Everyone loved him and he was a great favourite with mother's bed and breakfast guests. When Colin, my son, was born and we returned with him on holiday Ching followed him as he toddled around. When Colin was two years old, Ching patiently allowed Colin to play with him and even permitted him to pull his tail gently. He never snapped at him, but came to

*Ching with Grandma Eddy outside new porch*

me and, lying on my feet, looked at me with great sympathy as he realised I had to cope with an energetic little boy. We all missed Ching very much when he died.

### Cats

### Sandy

We had a cat called Sandy, a ginger tom, when I was about three and lived in London. I don't remember much about the first Sandy.

I remember our second Sandy when we lived in Mousehole. I played with him and dressed him in baby clothes. He replaced my dolls by being put in the pram and wheeled around Grandma's yard when she lived in 'Rosedene'. He only rebelled when I tried to feed him with the doll's feeding bottle! He preferred lapping his milk from a saucer. He was a lovely cat and lived to a great age.

### Tim

Tim was a black tom. I was then a teenager and valued his companionship. Dolls were now put aside as playthings for young children and I was interested in reading and playing the piano. Tim was always there – on my lap when I read and at my feet on a rug in the parlour when I practised the scales on the piano. I didn't take him for walks but he sat on the granite steps by the front door and welcomed me home from school and later on from my work in an office three miles away. I went by bus and he seemed to know the time and which bus I would be coming on. He had lovely yellow eyes and sleek fur. One of his paws was white and he had a white triangle on his chest. Of course, he followed me indoors when I arrived at teatime and I gave him his food and milk and listened to him purring contentedly.

One day he was sitting anxiously on the steps watching me walk up the hill towards our house. He mewed at me when I reached him and rubbed his head against my legs. I stroked him and he seemed nervous. Instead of coming indoors with me he turned away and, with tail erect, walked down the hill. I called to him but he did not turn his head. Instead he jumped the hedge leading to the fields leading to the rocks and sea. He ran away and that was the last time I saw him. He had waited for me to come home to say goodbye. A workman in the fields found his body later and it was thought that he had eaten some food contaminated with rat food, or perhaps he had eaten part of a poisoned rat. I grieved for my cat for many years.

*Budgies*

There was always a budgie in our house - a green one - and my mother taught Joey to speak. "He's a lovely boy!" he would state as he pulled on his bell and admired himself in the mirror hanging on the side of the cage. He was fun, but of course not a cuddly pet. One day he amazed all of us by saying, "Take his hand, Lily!" This was what Mother said to me every morning as I left for school with my young brother. Joey was a clever boy as he told everyone frequently.

*Goldfish*

Goldfish were popular and easy to feed. They just needed a sprinkle of their food on top of the water. If we could not be bothered to walk and brush a dog or cuddle a cat and feed it rabbit and liver we could easily look after the goldfish. I would beg rags from my family so that I could get a goldfish as payment from the rag and bone man. Sometimes I had the goldfish given to me in a tiny jar with very little water. The goldfish had to be transferred into a circular glass goldfish bowl. Some of my friends kept their fish in 2lb. jam jars. Of course we did not know how old or healthy the fish were so there were many deaths. Most of us put our dead fish in cardboard boxes and buried them with little ceremonies but there were few tears over a fish that just swam mechanically in circles during its short life.

# Village Life

*Food*

When I was growing up in Mousehole most cottages had an outside wall safe, a hanging box with a door covered in galvanised zinc mesh. This was fixed to a shaded wall and had one or two shelves. Food was stored in the 'safe' to keep it fresh. (There were no fridges in those childhood days.) Dried cod, known as 'tow rag' was hung on the wall beside it. Even the flies seemed to ignore this smelly food.

Grandpa Eddy had a lovely vegetable garden across the road from his cottage and provided us with blackcurrants, raspberries, rhubarb and apples, as well as the parsnips, carrots, beans and cabbages which he grew on this steep plot of land.

We went to the Kemyels to gather blackberries and my mother used them to make jam and blackberry and apple pies or crumbles. The blackberry picking was a family affair and we all tried to outdo one another, each wanting the most blackberries in their basket. It was a fun day and the nettles were treated by dock leaves wrapped around the sting. Cornish clotted cream topped the pies; we all wanted the cream with the yellow crust.

A pottery jug was left on the bottom granite step for the milkman to fill from his churn. A muslin bead-trimmed cover kept any dust from being blown into the milk. Before the war a vegetable and fruit man came to the door with his pony and trap and my brother and I were allowed to choose a fruit – I liked oranges and my brother loved bananas. Saffron cake was home-made and baked in the slab or taken to the village bakehouse.

Local men hunted rabbits which they delivered freshly killed. Grandpa skinned the rabbits, jointed them and put the joints in a bowl of water. They made wonderful stews for us at low cost.

*Lily and Derek waiting for the milk*

Pasties were eaten regularly. I liked the steak ones best of all. The best meat was skirt.

Swedes and carrots plus some onions gave moisture to the filling. Homemade pasties were lovely and everyone's tasted different: some people put a little kidney into theirs. Others liked to give their families lots of jammy maw – the standby bread and jam. Fresh homemade bread and homemade jam tasted delicious. We all loved bread with treacle and clotted cream – thunder and lightning. My grandfather liked homemade bread – sops – in milk and soup. And my father liked sops in his gravy. Grandma pickled eggs and marinated pilchards. Heavy or hevva cake was always made for the fishermen coming ashore with a good catch. I loved this - it was rich and fruity - really heavy. Fried fresh mackerel, straight from the fishing harbour, was just wonderful. Fresh white fish was often eaten with a dippy sauce and this white sauce was good too, especially with mashed potatoes, the potatoes grown in grandpa's garden.

Grandpa Eddy sometimes prepared crabs for our meals. I hated hearing the singing noise from the crabs boiling on the kitchen slab. Occasionally I was given the claws, which I cracked with a hammer on our garden steps. The fresh meat from these claws was very tasty; however, I obtained very little meat from the smaller legs, but it was fun extracting what I could from them with a meat skewer.

Although the war with Germany ended in May 1945, rationing continued for some years, and we were grateful for the parcels we received from relatives in Canada.

*Clothes*

During my childhood we had a visiting dressmaker called Jane. She was very popular and when a special dress or outfit was needed she would come for the day and have her meals with us. My mother took extra care making our meals that day.

Jane was lame and did not move around with ease, so my younger brother was delighted to pick up the pins she dropped, fairly frequently, from the floor.

I remember making sketches for her and she made up clothes from my descriptions – shirred elastic waistlines were popular. Many pins were used to save time in tacking.

During the war years she used 'turned' material into smaller coats, skirts and pinafore dresses, especially for the children. Grandma, who lived next door to us, supplied the hand Singer sewing machine. Grandma made simple blouses for all of us and turned my father's shirt collars and cuffs when they frayed, especially during the years of rationing and coupons. We had special dresses every year for Sunday School Anniversary, which came at Whitsun. If possible, the dress was made from white material.

My clothes for Chapel-going included a hat, gloves, stockings or white socks and leather or black patent leather shoes; the shoes were 'best' shoes and kept for Sunday wear. We went for walks for recreation and our heels were often rubbed and blistered after a long walk on a hot day. Summer hats were often made of straw and decorated with artificial fruits and flowers.

I had a 'best dress' every year as most other village girls had. This was worn on Sundays and during our growing years was too small for 'best' after one season. Often it was too tight to be worn for second 'best' as well, so was passed on to relatives to wear. I remember my chagrin and that of my parents when one distant cousin was seen wearing my favourite good quality discarded 'best' turquoise dress to go on blackberrying expeditions! I had not been allowed to wear it for a party – Sunday Chapel only.

When I went to parties I wore an artificial flower in my hair. Grandma had given me a very nice white camellia, which she had worn as a buttonhole arrangement at a special event. Party-time meant I could borrow mother's jewellery – the inexpensive pretty glass beads and bracelets mainly. Shoes were patent leather with a strap across the front of the foot which kept the shoe from slipping. I can still remember having blisters if I walked too far in those shoes.

There was a shoe shop, 'Jolliffe's', in our village and ordinary lace-up shoes were bought there. 'Best' shoes were bought in town, which was three miles away and meant a ride on the local bus. Sometimes dresses were bought in town and we knew the owner of the shop personally.

Occasionally we would have a parcel from America containing cousins' cast-offs. We liked receiving these and, if they fitted us, we wore the clothes with pride.

When I was a young child my dresses had frills from the waist to the hemline and we loved to follow the styles of the Princesses Elizabeth and Margaret Rose.

I did not have a bra until I was well into my teens but wore a liberty bodice. It seemed popular to hide the bosoms rather than emphasize them as happens now. My stockings were held up by garters of pieces of elastic which dug into my thighs. Sometimes, in winter, long suspenders were clipped on to the bottom of my liberty bodice to hold up my stockings. If a parcel from America contained nylons we were in seventh heaven.

Cami-knickers (wide leg panties) were fashionable. Pure silk ones trimmed with lovely lace came from America.

My first bathing costume was knitted in wool by my Auntie Phyllis. It became very heavy when wet and took ages to dry. I remember that later on shirred elastic cotton costumes were fashionable.

Hats came in fashion, always worn with matching gloves. I had a pillbox hat in navy, a Deanna Durban hat in brown felt and a Scottish beret shape hat with a lovely pheasant's feather across the right hand side. Veils of eye length were pretty and my straw hats were white with artificial flowers and fruits. I admired but did not own a hat trimmed with a small felt bird.

I did not have professional perms for my hair, as it was naturally wavy. I wore it 'bob' length, just above the shoulders. When I washed my hair - 'Friday night was shampoo night' - I sometimes used 'dinky' curlers. These were metal and very uncomfortable for wearing overnight – sleep was very disturbed. Haircuts were rare events.

*Cures*

There was a medicine cupboard in our kitchen with mother's family cures. It contained Aspirin for colds and headaches and Iodine for cuts and scrapes. There were bandages, lint and cotton wool.

The Friar's Balsam Jug stood on a shelf. It was a small blue narrow-necked jug, which I inherited. If anyone in the family had a cold or sore throat, the blue jug would be filled with near boiling water and a few drops from the Friar's Balsam bottle were added. The patient then sat huddled over the jug, with a towel covering the head, inhaling the vapour.

Camphorated oil was another cold cure. Mother warmed a little oil on a saucer, either on top of the slab or in its oven. This was slapped on our backs and chests: sometimes it was too hot for comfort. The aroma was pleasant to me and certainly helped clear congestion. Hot lemon drinks made from squeezed fresh lemons were also considered a cure for sore throats.

In winter I had a dessertspoonful of Cod Liver Oil and Malt every day. There was as much mixture on top of the spoon as inside it. The taste was palatable but the amount of the mixture took a while to swallow. However, this was taken to prevent colds from developing or even preventing them from starting at all.

The Syrup of Figs administered for constipation was not an acceptable flavour to me but usually frightened the system to return to normal. A blue bag was always on hand for bee stings and vinegar for wasp stings.

A bread poultice, which was a piece of bread soaked in boiling water tied up in a piece of sheeting and then squeezed to extract surplus water, was placed on boils or sores. This had to be as hot as bearable and was used to extract 'pus'. It worked, but sometimes sensitive skin suffered blisters. I also had kaolin poultices applied to large boils which developed under my arm when I was a teenager. This poultice was a china clay mixture in a tin. The tin was heated and the sticky mixture spread on a piece of linen and slapped on the boil. Agony, but it worked.

There was no National Health Service and doctors' fees were avoided when simple remedies could be used for common ailments. Sometimes the boils refused to go away and needed lancing, so a visit to the Doctor's surgery was inevitable.

One day at teatime I was cutting bread for the family and the knife I was using slipped and cut into the index finger of my left hand. Mother was in bed and unwell at the time and Father had just arrived home, so by the time he came into the kitchen, there was blood flowing from my finger and I could see bits inside the finger. The cotton wool and bandages were brought into service and wrapped around my finger. They did not stop the bleeding and, according to our neighbour, stitches were needed. We had no car or telephone and had just missed the bus to the Lariggan in Newlyn where the Doctor had his surgery. So Father and I walked there - distance of two and a half miles. I needed six stitches and had, we were told, just missed slicing through the ligament. I had lost quite a lot of blood and did not want to walk back again. My arm was put in a sling and I was told not to use my hand for at least ten days and then the stitches would be removed.

We walked back to Newlyn Bridge (some 400 yards) and waited for the service bus back to Mousehole. Being 'tough' was the order of the day and nobody thought of having a taxi for an 'excursion' to the Doctor.

I was lucky in that I healed up well. I can still see the scar left by that accident.

We had a resident nurse in Mousehole – Nurse Pender, who lived near the Post Office. I remember visiting her for consultations on minor complaints. She removed splinters, attended to sore knees from falls in our gravel covered school playground and gave advice on small cuts and bruises. Nurse Pender was an efficient but stern lady.

*Code of behaviour*

At school we were taught local history so we knew that the Keigwin Arms was a pub many years ago. It was the last house to be left standing when the Spaniards raided Mousehole in 1595. At that time, we were told, the villagers fled to Paul and took refuge in the Church.

We illustrated our stories in history lessons and this was a good way of remembering both local and general events in history. One such story was the Merry Maidens being turned into stone because they danced on a Sunday. The pipers ran off and they were turned into standing stones in the nearby fields. This was folklore and local history mixed together and a lesson in behaviour because Sundays were treated as holy days in my childhood. Not even boats were put to sea for fishing. It was considered bad behaviour to set foot on the beach and enjoy games. Of course, not everyone obeyed these rules, but most Chapel folk did. Sundays were for Chapel, morning and evening and Sunday School, morning and afternoon. Grandpa Eddy paid seat rent for a well-positioned pew in the centre of the gallery at St. Clement's, so I always sat there. I had my own music edition hymn book of which I was very proud.

My Grandma Eddy would not allow even sewing to be done on Sundays. Playing games, especially if they involved playing cards, which were the 'work of the Devil', was frowned upon. No housework was done on Sundays, except for the preparation of meals. That sort of work was considered important. After all, the men required their Sunday roasts of meat, potatoes and at least two vegetables. Fruit, tinned when available, or rice pudding would follow this. My brother and I were instructed to eat every scrap of our dinners before we were allowed to eat the dessert.

*Charming, Folklore and Superstitions*

Men walked on the 'Cliff' overlooking the harbour. It was a measured distance each way – almost like line dancing. It was said that the old fishermen walked the length of a boatdeck, turned, and walked the same length again and again. There were several groups, each with their own section of the Cliff. Even if the men did not join in the walking, they stood on the Cliff in groups to gossip or just look at the boats, the sea and the quays of the harbour.

The village charmer spent most of his time on the Cliff and one day a schoolfriend suggested that I should ask him to 'charm' my wart. His name was Bert Jenkin and I hated my wart which stood up on my knuckle. I had tried to get rid of it myself by rubbing it with fresh steak which was then buried under a window in my Granny's small front garden. The wart was supposed to disappear when the meat rotted but it did not. I had also taken the ninth pea from a pod containing nine peas and threw the pea away, saying, 'Wart, wart, dry away!' but it did not. So I was pushed towards Bertie Jenkin and my friend stood by me and told the 'charmer' about my wart. He took my hand in his and put his fingers on my wart. Then, with his eyes turned towards the sky, he said words – an incantation I did not understand. I remember that his eyes were very blue. Then he closed them for a moment. "Do you believe?" he asked me. "Yes", I murmured. I really did. "Then, it will go," he said. And it did and never came back again. Magic? It seemed to be to me. However, I did have faith. I believe Mr. Jenkin was the last of the 'Charmers'.

The fishermen had many superstitions regarding their boats and going to sea. It was considered very unlucky to mention rabbits, hares and other wild animals when at sea. If these animals had to be mentioned, then they were referred to as 4-leggers or 2-deckers. Whistling was forbidden as it was said that whistling at sea would 'whistle up the wind'. A priest or minister was known as a 'white choker'. If a fisherman met a parson on his way to his boat, he considered it a very unlucky occurrence and he would not go to sea that day. It was also considered ill luck to meet a woman when going to fish and when shoals of mullet were sighted close inshore, the women were sent indoors until the catch was landed. Perhaps this was the old fishermen's way of keeping the women at home baking the hevva cake, pasties, saffron cakes and ginger fairings!!

Pieces of clothes from people needing a cure from an illness were hung on bushes around holy wells. The nearest well to us was at Madron, and I remember seeing the torn pieces of clothing when we went there.

Children with rickets were taken to the Men-an-Tol (the stone with a hole) on the moors above Madron. They were passed three times, preferably backwards, through the circle stone as a cure for this disease, but I did not know of anyone who had this treatment.

My Grandpa would not allow bluebells to be brought indoors. He called them 'cuckoos'. Maythorn was also forbidden indoors. It was considered unlucky to spill salt. If we spilled salt on the dining table, we had to take a pinch of that salt between the thumb and first finger of our right hand and throw the salt over the left shoulder. I remember that our grandmothers said that it was very unlucky to wash blankets in May month, and that if knives were crossed in the laying of a table, there would soon be a quarrel. If clothing was put on inside out, it had to remain that way. To change a garment back would mean losing luck. Wearing green was also considered unlucky by Cornish folk.

In Spring, when the shoots were fresh on the bushes and trees, we used to chew the tender leaves of the hawthorn, which we called 'bread and cheese'. We also chewed the fresh leaves of sorrel and these were known as 'soursops'. Another custom was the making of peashooters by the boys from the long stems of hogweed. The pith was easily removed and the hard unripe fruit of elderberries made excellent peas. The girls suffered from the peashooting attacks.

In our teens we tried to peel apples or oranges on the round keeping the whole peel in one continuous strip. If successful, this was then thrown over the left shoulder. It was believed that when it landed the peel would form the shape of the initial of the Christian name of the man you would marry.

I remember even in childhood the custom of receiving a large apple known as an 'Allan' apple and putting it under my pillow was very pleasant. This took place on the Saturday evening nearest to Hallowe'en on the 31st October. It was supposed to bring peace to the owner, but it was there to be eaten in the morning. Later on, in my teens, I hoped that the apple under the pillow overnight would make me dream and see the person who would become my sweetheart.

Whenever someone said something obvious or ridiculous, it was said to be like something done by Jan Stone. The story goes that he couldn't find a pair of size 14 shoes in Penzance, so he bought two pairs of size 7. Another saying was that he went to his place of employment to tell them that he was poorly and couldn't come to work that day. I remember my mother and grandmother admonishing us when we said something silly, "You're as bad as Jan Stone!"

*Going Visiting*

A favourite pastime during childhood days was visiting relatives. Perhaps I should say that this was the grownups' pleasure; I was just taken along.

Grandma Eddy visited Aunt Alberta who was Miss Cumberland's housekeeper. Occasionally I went along too and shared a cake and drank a cup of tea with Aunt Alberta in the kitchen. This was a pleasant visit and included a walk along Love Lane where the house was situated. There was a pretty flower garden and I wandered there while the ladies had their gossip. Sometimes we visited Aunt Alberta in her own home, which was situated at the bottom of Old Hill near St. Clement's Chapel. We climbed up steep steps to the front door of the house or up the steep beginning of Old Hill to her back door. I remember going through her large cellar at this entrance and through to the kitchen.

Our family visited Grandpa Eddy's brother Will and his wife and daughters at Lamorna. This involved a two mile walk there and back. They had a nice garden and the girls played games with me there. Sometimes we walked to Lamorna from the Crackers and along the footpath, across fields, and then through the three farms known as the Kemyels.

My father loved visiting family and friends, so I was taken to Aunt Amelia Polgrean who lived in Newlyn at the top of Newlyn Slip. This was a two mile walk through Mousehole past Penlee Point with the Lifeboat House and then past the 'Welsh' houses to continue through the eerie Penlee Quarry. Aunt Amelia received us in her front room. We sat on upright dining room chairs and drank our tea from her best china cups.

Another visit was to Aunt Deborah Polgrean who lived in a terrace of houses across the 'Bank' above the first cove. I walked between hedges of what we called 'boys' love'. I pressed a sprig through my fingers to release the aromatic herby smell.

I was never sure of our relationship to other people we visited but we were encouraged to call them Auntie and Uncle!

Short holidays were spent with Grandpa's sister Grace Richards in Ponsanooth. Her family lived with her or in the next door house and it was a good holiday break for my mother. Houses in country areas usually had earth toilets in the garden years ago. These were known as 'privvies'. I was not happy at sitting on a wooden seat over a bucket, or over an earth pit lined with bracken in some cases.

I was sitting on the top of the garden gate at my Aunt's cottage where our family were staying. It was twilight and I was alone in the quietness of a late Spring evening, just looking at the flowers in the hedge on the other side of the main road which ran through the village. Suddenly, a sleek black car came down the hillside and, as it approached me, it suddenly stopped. I watched a man get out of the car and walk towards me. Then, another man got out and followed him. There was something  sinister about the way they looked up and down the road. No one was about. They both held out their arms to me. Instinct told me that they were dangerous. I jumped off the gate and ran back down the path to the cottage and scraped my leg in doing so. The men stood and watched me for a moment and I heard them say, "Let's go!" They hurried to their car and scrambled inside.

My mother listened to my story and told me that I had done the right thing in running away. I had not been watching TV - there was none in those days - and I had not been reading horror stories. The men may have been innocent, but I still remember that my heart stood still at the way they acted.

However, country food was always good - home-made saffron cake was delicious. One day mother's cousin had her cake 'proving' in the parlour on a chair covered by a tea towel. I did not notice the basin and sat on the rising yeast mixture. It was not rising any more when I jumped up and I was told that I had ruined that batch of saffron cake!

My only horse ride was at a farm near Porkellis when a relative of Phyllis' mother had holidays in one of the farm cottages and I was staying there too. On this occasion my heart stood still when Phyllis' cousin who had helped me get on a farm horse gave the horse a whack to make it move and sent it cantering down the lane with me riding bareback and clinging on to its mane. I couldn't stop the animal and felt myself gradually slipping off. I screamed and screamed and eventually the lad caught up with us and managed to bring the horse to a halt. I had thought this lad very handsome and was a little attracted to him until he played this prank on me!

## Outings

Early outings were with parents and relatives. We lived up the steep Raginnis Hill about 100 yards from St. Clement's Chapel and a shop. As we were not actually in the village a visit to the beach was an outing, especially as it involved a walk through the narrow streets of Mousehole past quaint shops and the harbour colourful with boats. The boats were owned by villagers and most of them were shared by families. Most men owned a punt used for fishing or just for rowing to the Island for fun. Grandpa owned a punt - the 'Springbok' - and he also shared a motor boat with another man: this boat was the 'Diamond'.

Mother, father, Grandma and Grandpa Eddy, baby brother Derek and myself had a wonderful outing to St. Michael's Mount transported by the 'Diamond'. Other relatives and friends and Grandma's dog Dinkie accompanied us. Aunt Alberta and Auntie Sarah Wright, Grandma's friends, came and are part of the group in the photograph which was taken. I remember that brother Derek needed a feed and mother wanted to warm the milk she had brought with her. She knocked on the door of one of the cottages which

*Our group on St Michael's Mount*

stood on the harbour front and asked the old lady who answered the door if she would kindly warm the bottle of milk she had so that she could feed Derek with milk of the right temperature. She willingly let us into her spotlessly clean living room where a fire was burning in the small basket grate. A clean saucepan was produced and the milk was poured into it. The saucepan went on the live coals and the milk was brought to boiling point. It was then cooled a little and the feeding bottle was filled and baby Derek had his feed. She was a lovely old lady.

Later on we went back to the boat and motored back to Mousehole harbour. It was an outing to remember.

I went with Grandma Eddy and Grandpa in the 'Springbok' to St. Clement's Island. Grandpa rowed, of course, and we all fished for mackerel with feathers after we had anchored by the island. When we got back home again the fresh fish we had caught were cleaned and fried and eaten with bread and butter. Wonderful!

Family picnics were popular before the Second World War. I never had a picnic on the Island but was told that many people did so. Their transport

*Family picnic at the Battery*
*Father in charge of the kettle*

was a punt or motor boat well packed with crockery, primus stove, white linen table cloth, cushions and food. I did have a picnic at the 'Battery' and the equipment was transported by the men in wicker clothes flaskets and we walked along the pathway to the cliffs known as the 'Cave Rocks'. The food included home-made pasties and saffron cake. Heavy or 'heva' cake and caraway seed cake were also favourites.

The daisy field or 'Uncle Fred's field' up the 'Mountains' (the end of Love Lane) was another picnic place where there was plenty of room for games or the creation of daisy chains. There were reeds at the bottom of the field and artificial roses were fashioned from the pith.

Most families walked from Mousehole to Lamorna on Good Friday. The reason for visiting Lamorna is not known but it is still a pilgrimage on that day. Daffodils and primroses were gathered on the way. When we got to the Cove at Lamorna we sat on rocks and the small quay or had tea in the grassy gardens outside the cottages on the front. A happy social occasion.

The Mousehole Sunday Schools organised outings to nearby seaside places by charabanc. The journeys were as much fun as the venues. The excitement started as we walked up to the Parade to the waiting large buses. (The buses were too long to come around the corners to the harbour.) A tea was arranged at the destination and included a large teatreat saffron bun for each child and a bottle of pop which had a glass marble stopper. The teachers looked after the children, and parents could also go along if they wished to do so. Games and races were the entertainment.

In wartime Galas were held in a local field instead of the outings by bus. A brass or silver band led the procession of walkers and large banners were carried to the chosen spot and teas, games and races were arranged by the teachers. The older boys and girls played 'Kiss in the ring' which was very popular!

*Speedboat ahoy! Roma Bale, Lily Polgrean, Audrey Eddy, Thelma Eddy*

Choir outings from St. Clement's Church and Mount Zion Church were a little more sophisticated, but all went by bus and had either a picnic or tea at the venue. On one outing to Looe a group of us girls teamed up and we had our first ever ride in a speedboat. Very exciting!

Relatives came to Cornwall for their holidays and the children in the host families were sometimes taken on outings by them. Uncle Will, my father's half-brother, and his wife Auntie Rene, took me on outings to St. Ives with their children Phyllis and Harry. I remember that on one occasion Phyllis and I hired a sea float and Phyllis, who was four years older than me, was in charge of the paddle. All went well until Harry, who was older than Phyllis, tipped up our float. I fell off and can still remember the sensation of breathlessness as my head went under the water. Terrible stifling feelings, but Harry rescued me so a tragedy was avoided. After this outing Phyllis taught me to swim in the Round Pool in Mousehole Cove.

Another outing with Uncle Will to Land's End ended with Uncle Will's car half way over a hedge, but the right way up. Derek and I returned to Mousehole on a milk float.

On another occasion we went to Phyllis' cousin's farm. We were staying a few nights in a farm cottage with no running water in the bedroom for washing ourselves. There was no bathroom, so Auntie Rene had filled a jug with water and it stood on a small stand which held a basin with a plug and chain attached to it. This basin was in a hole in the top of the stand. After my first wash I pulled out the plug from the basin and all the water ran on to the floor. I had not realised that the bucket beneath the basin was missing! I was horrified and very apologetic, but I did not escape a scolding or the chore of mopping up the water!

When on holiday to Zennor we met Marie Kliskey, and my brother and I went to 'Eagle's Nest' where Marie's mother was housekeeper. We had tea with her in the kitchen. I remember we roamed the moors opposite the big house and we were intrigued by an empty isolated cottage there. We thought this cottage was haunted and treated it with respect. My brother, Derek, was much younger than us and he still remembers being frightened when Marie and I wandered off, leaving him alone in the cottage for a short while. There were peculiar noises sounding from the large chimney. There was always a stray black cat near the cottage and the whole atmosphere was very creepy and cold.

When I was five years old my lovely eccentric Auntie Phyllis (my father's half-sister) took me to the pebble beach at Penzance which was very popular years ago. There was a water slide and I climbed up the ladder and went down the slide with ease. Later, I went to the slide again but did not realise that the tide had come up, filling the hole made at the bottom of the slide. Luckily I was rescued by a lady who had been swimming. She caught me in her arms and marched up the beach to where Auntie Phyllis was snoozing and gave her a lecture on looking after children in dangerous places. After that, outings to Penzance with Auntie Phyllis were confined to the Morrab Gardens where we took bread to feed birds and played a game trying to catch a bird by putting salt on its tail.

I enjoyed going to the large Corpus Christi Fair which came to Penzance every Whitsun. I remember the thrill of riding on the 'Big Wheel' and marvelling at the wonderful view of Penzance from the top of the wheel. The sweet stalls were fabulous – my favourites were the reels of 'wacko', a sticky toffee, cream and burnt sienna in colour. Winter green sweets, hot mint and cinnamon flavours were good and the cheaper liquorice assortments were always acceptable!


*Wartime Holiday*

Our family loved going to Zennor for a holiday. We stayed in a friend's chalet. This was in the garden near a greenhouse of colourful summer plants and as a child I was delighted to have the privilege to help with the watering. The perfumes of the flowers were wonderful.

From Zennor St. Ives was accessible by catching a bus from the village stop, or by walking through fields and moorland. I walked to St. Ives and back to Zennor again many times with father, who loved a good walk.

At St. Ives the bus stop near to the beautiful sandy beach was called the Malakoff and from here we had a lovely view of the St. Ives' harbour. Returning from the beach to catch a bus home again, parents and children were tired but happy with sand-sprinkled buckets and spades - except for one day during World War Two. That day children and frightened parents, carrying buckets holed by bullets, crowded to the buses to be comforted by the bus conductors and drivers.

This particular day (August 28th 1942) my mother, myself and younger brother had left Zennor on the bus to St. Ives carrying sandwiches for lunch and towels and swimming gear. We soon found a spot on the beach and carefree families soon crowded around us. The sun glistened on the sea inviting me and some others to get into the water. After swimming and splashing around it seemed time to get back to family groups. I had drifted along the beach and found that I had a longer walk back than I had expected. The sun had disappeared and being wet without a towel I felt chilly. I threaded my way through the crowds looking for my mother. Suddenly there was the drone of an aeroplane and I noted that it was flying very low over the beach. I knew little about aeroplanes but felt alarmed to see something dropping from beneath the plane. Instinct made me run to the concrete shelters which were mainly used as changing areas. Hardly noticing the wall in front of them I jumped it and was one of the first to run inside a shelter.

The plane turned back to the beach. The bombs had dropped near the town, but the plane then started to machine-gun the beach. It completed the length and then disappeared. I got out af the shelter - I had to find my mother and brother. I stumbled through the frightened crowds who were looking for their families.

At last I found my mother. She had straddled my brother in her efforts to protect him. We followed the people who were now rushing along the beach and back to the Malakoff. There were many holed buckets on the sands, but no wounded people. Shock had replaced everyone's happiness.

The Malakoff was in chaos. There were so many brave people protecting their families. Apparently one bomb had dropped near the Gasworks and caused some damage. People on Porthmeor beach were injured by debris and shrapnel. It was a miracle, they all said, that no person was injured or killed on Porthminster. Yes, it was - but it was an experience imprinted on the mind for ever.

My mother fainted only when reaching the chalet at Zennor.

The holiday ended and we went back home to safety and the metal Morrison table shelter in our kitchen.

Yes, we did use the shelter. Mv brother and I slept in the shelter when the bombs were dropped in a field opposite Paul Church, and when Mousehole Island (St. Clement's Isle) was machine-gunned by mistake for a warship. Gunfire was very frightening, especially at night time, but our mother was always there to comfort us.

My childhood was enhanced by these memories.

My cousin Harry was in the RAF in the war and was a flight gunner in Halifaxes. Sadly he was shot down over Hamburg just a week before flying operations ended in March 1945.

# Festivals

*May Day in the early 40's*

May Day in Cornwall was an important occasion, not only in Padstow, but in all the villages of Cornwall where we celebrated the coming of Spring.

On May Day morning the young people of Mousehole would gather (up the Curtis) with the girls dressed in long skirts and white net curtains and appoint a girl as leader of the group (latterly known as the 'May Queen'). She would gather around her in Queen Bee fashion her attendants and the followers who would process through the village streets. The boys blew tin May horns kept just for this day and May whistles home-made from sycamore bark. Sycamore branches would be stripped of bark by cutting a ring through the bark at a short distance from the end of the branch. The bark was then slipped off the branch and a hole was made in the hollow pipe which became a whistle. The group was known as the May Band. Some gathered May blossom (hawthorn), the girls making garlands for good luck. (The actual May was sycamore, not hawthorn). The May Band gathered again at an appointed spot, usually the Old Quay, and then dispersed. The boys were very proud of their May horns and of the whistles that were cut freshly each year. The May (Sycamore) gathered was welcome in houses, but not the May blossom, as the descendants of the fisher folk considered hawthorn 'poor luck' when brought indoors. I remember that my May blossom had to remain out of doors in a jar of water. The 1st Penzance Company of the GLB revived the custom of having a May Queen, processing through the village from St. Clement's Sunday School Hall. In my time, the village never had a maypole.

Ancient folk tradition states that May Day had a special significance as the day when witches had special power. It was believed that the May music was to scare away these evil spirits from the dwellings of the just.

Placing green boughs over doorways was generally believed to give luck – or that the spirit of vegetation in the boughs would bring blessing on the house.

*Christmas at Mousehole*

Christmas was exciting to me when I was young. There was the preparation first of all. The learning of carols, rehearsals for concerts, making decorations and cards were enjoyable. Present buying, bazaars, helping stir the pudding and taking cakes to the bake-house all added excitement to the proceedings.

On one or two evenings before Christmas Eve, and on the Eve itself, the Chapel Choirs would go Carol Singing – one or two evenings in the village, and then up Raginnis Hill, on through farms to Sheffield and back down through Paul. These often went on until after midnight and I found them uplifting and thrilling when I was old enough to go along. There were usually at least thirty people and the singing was in full four-part harmony with one or two local favourites (especially Merritt's carols) and tunes I have not heard elsewhere.

After opening my stocking (or pillowcase!) on Christmas morning, I went to Chapel for the Service. Afterwards, I delivered presents and cards to my friends. Christmas Day dinner was with my parents, grandparents and any aunts or friends who were staying with us. After turkey, goose or duck with all the trimmings, came the pudding with clotted cream or custard. This was eaten carefully because I had to find the threepenny bit or sixpenny piece which would be hidden inside. Hot mincepies followed if anyone still had room in their tummies. Crackers were pulled and fancy hats worn for the rest of the day.

After clearing the table and washing the dirty dishes we played games. We unwrapped and played with our presents. Even 'I Spy' was exciting in the atmosphere. The Christmas tree lights always fused at one point, but nobody felt too upset. The tree was of Cornish holly, very prickly!

The Christmas cake was cut at teatime, and we ate sausage rolls and more mince pies. At supper time we had ham sandwiches with an assortment of pickles, and pickled onions. Tea, ginger wine and lemonade were offered to the guests before they went back to their own homes.

Boxing Day was for visiting friends and walking. We usually had cold meat at lunch time. I have walked to Trevelloe Carn to catch sight of the Boxing Day Hunt. If someone had a car, we went to Madron to see the Hunt gather. All the scarlet coats were very attractive.

In the evening friends would meet up for a party, and more food. Left over turkey, chicken or ham were made into delicious sandwiches, and once again, there would be mincepies.

Next day, it was back to work again for the workers. There were no long holidays from offices and shops in those days. But Christmas fun was not at an end. There were still Sunday School and Chapel Socials to enjoy. Games played at these socials were musical chairs, postman's knock, passing the orange under the chin without using the hands. This was our chance to put our arms around the boys! There was also 'Spin the plate' and a variation 'Spin the bottle' and 'Winking', which was a problem if one had not mastered the art! Then we passed a ring under our hands around a loop of string and if the ring was in your possession when the person in the middle of the room pointed at you, you had to pay a forfeit. Fine if you were an accomplished member and could sing, dance or recite a poem.

When I was very young, a few people still went 'Guise Dancing', and this gradually died out during the 30's. But I can still remember small groups of people who continued the custom. The men dressed as women and the women dressed as men, all in old-fashioned clothes. Some wore small eye masks. These people knocked on village doors and asked for refreshments, all the while concealing their identity. They were given Christmas cake and ginger wine or tea. My Grandma was delighted to receive her visitors, as she was always ready to keep up traditions. The 'Guise Dancers' usually rewarded the providers of food by performing a little dance, sometimes to a drum and mouth organ accompaniment.

The ginger wine, so popular in the village at Christmas, was made from a Newlyn Chemist's 'best' ginger wine essence mixed in a large bowl with sugar and hot water. The non-alcoholic brew was then bottled. Sometimes my mother and grandmother added lemonade as well. This was offered to all visitors during the Christmas and New Year festivities.

One year, I well remember that Mother had a goose for Christmas. Although she took the plucking of a chicken in her stride, the goose was a different matter. As the feathers flew around the kitchen as Mother plucked the bird, she vowed never to have a goose again. It had been a mammoth task.

# Teenage years

Our childhood friendships continued. New friendships were made, we noticed boys and, with the war, there were restrictions in our lives. We carried identity cards, grey blue in colour, we needed ration books for food and had coupons for buying clothes. We carried gasmasks everywhere we went.

Food which usually came from overseas countries started disappearing from shops. We queued for dried bananas occasionally obtainable from a shop in Causewayhead, Penzance. Petrol was rationed so cars for pleasure were few. Priorities were introduced and petrol was allowed for cars used for 'essential' work. Petrol rationing lasted ten years until 1950.

We lived under the threat of bombs and invasion by the enemy. The important beaches had wire fencing and some of them had land mines planted as defence.

Songs were sung as morale boosters and we learned these songs sung by Vera Lynn and many others when they were entertaining the troops. I played the songs on the piano from 6d. sheet music and learnt the words and music. Healthy teenagers from seventeen years upwards were 'called up' for service in the armed forces. Some girls went into the Land Army as it was important to grow our own food to supplement our diet,

Strangers who now came to Mousehole were considered as suspicious as 'they might be spies for the enemy'. 'Careless talk costs lives' was a saying we all took seriously. We were also warned not to accept gifts, including sweets, from strangers. Locally, we had the Home Guard to protect us. The Captain was Edwin Waters who was in charge of the local volunteers dressed in army uniform. Other volunteers acted as Air Raid Wardens and they appeared during air raid alerts.

During the war, almost all local families earned a little extra money by making camouflage nets. These were taken to a local fish cellar where one of the village fishermen inspected the work. It was quickly rejected if not absolutely perfect, with regular meshes and tight knots.

Red Cross nurse training was based in the British Legion Hall in Mousehole village. We took instruction here to learn bandaging and first aid. I obtained my Girls' Life Brigade First Aid badge in this way. The British Legion Hall was a building with a nice stage at one end where plays were performed. The Boys' Brigade and Girls' Life Brigade got together to act in one of them. Games were available for use in the hall, and some evening dances were held. I did go to one of these dances, just to watch the goings on, with Thelma Eddy. Her parents went too, but my parents did not like me to go to these quite innocent occasions and the only time I went, my father came along at 8.30 pm and hauled me out and home. I did protest that these 'goings on' were quite innocent, but to no avail.

I became a Sunday School teacher at the age of fifteen or sixteen and loved telling stories from the Bible to the beginners' class. We had sand trays and used clean wooden meat skewers for drawing pictures in the sand. I remember that I still have a little serpentine rock with a brass pixie on top which one of the children gave to me when I married. I attended a Bible Study class taken by Mrs. Williams, Beryl's mother.

Along with my friends, I auditioned for St. Clement's Church Choir. We were readily received. I sat on the alto side and we went along to choir practice every week and sang in the choir on Sundays. At Christmas we sang carols in the Concert. At Easter, we sang 'Olivet to Calvary' alternately with the 'Crucifixion'. On special occasions, we sang 'Messiah'. Most of us could read music as we studied the piano, so it was a pleasure to fit it all in.

My father, Arnold Polgrean, had formed the village company of the Boys' Brigade with Mr Fox in 1933 and this was well established. When my friends were about thirteen, we decided that we wanted an organization for girls. We wanted Girl Guides or ATS which we had heard about, or the Girls' Life Brigade. Mrs Doris Richards, from Paul, was a Methodist Minister's wife and her husband was serving in the forces during the war, so in 1944, a group of girls, myself included, approached her to ask if she would run an organization for the girls. She agreed to start a Girls' Life Brigade Company, which became the 1st Penzance Company and I was a founder member, rising through the ranks to Lieutenant under a later Captain, Mrs. Janie Pender.

When the Boys' Brigade Company camped at Hayle many of the parents of the boys went to the Open Day. I went along with some friends and we had a special bus to take us to Hayle. My brother Derek, who was five years younger than I was, went along as well, so it was an all-age outing. When the GLB went on outings to nearby seaside towns some of the village boys came too. We were all good friends.

During the war, a company of soldiers had their camp in a field at Raginnis, which was just above us at the top of the hill and just outside the village. My father, who remembered his days serving in the Army in Ireland

*BB Open Day at Hayle Towans.*

*Captain Arnold Polgrean extreme top left*

*GLB and friends at St Ives with Mrs Doris Richards*
*(l. to r.) Front row: Pam Hocking, Ann Quick, Ruth Pomeroy, Mrs Doris Richards (Captain), Maureen Richards, Pamela Howe, Estelle Wallis Middle Row: (?), Sylvia Pender, Jean Brownfield, Thelma Eddy, Lily Polgrean, Kathleen Hall, Myra Humphries, Roma Bale, Jean Wallis Back row: Ruth Downing, Beryl Williams, Pentreath Johns, Clifton Pender, Joe Gilbert, Hugh Sampson, Barbara Eddy*

and in Germany immediately after the First World War, would often befriend some of the soldiers. A cup of tea and a chat or a light meal meant a lot to some of them. One day, four of them hired a punt to go to Mousehole Island. They landed there and found that the seagulls were nesting and they gathered many eggs. They brought the eggs to my mother with the request that she cooked them for their supper. She fried them for them and supplied toast and bread as well. However, the eggs smelled and tasted strongly of fish and mother had to discard her frying pan and buy a new one. The soldiers enjoyed the experience of eating their fish flavoured eggs and washed the food down with many cups of tea. One airman whom we befriended became a friend for life. He kept in touch with the family and visited us after the war.

Carnivals have always taken place in the summer in Cornish villages. The GLB entered the Mousehole Carnivals and decorated their lorry with greenery and flowers. Hydrangeas were plentiful and grew wild in some fields so were good decorating material. I remember two Carnivals in particular in which I took part. In one I was Titania in 'A Midsummer Night's Dream' and in another I was the bride in 'The Bride wore Boots', a popular musical at the time. It was great fun going through the village with a brass or silver band leading the Parade. We sometimes ended by driving to Penzance and parading through the town. Our Carnival Queen was so pretty that she frequently went on to be chosen as Miss Cornwall.

*GLB Carnival float*

Bert Dyer made a copper crown for the Carnival Queen. He was a very talented coppersmith who worked in the tradition of the acclaimed Newlyn Copper. Herbert Victor, who lived near him in the Millpool area, was an artist excelling in watercolours. Jack Pender, brother of my friend Sylvia, painted Cornish scenes and his work was much sought after and bought by many famous people.

There were two Methodist Chapels in Mousehole at this time and I had friends in both – the BB and GLB had boys and girls from both Chapels and

*'A Midsummer Night's Dream' on its way through the village*

they met in St. Clement's Sunday School Hall. This was the Wesleyan Chapel and was always referred to as 'Down Chapel'. 'Up Chapel' was Mount Zion and there was a friendly rivalry between them. We attended each other's annual teas, concerts and special Services, although on the night before each Chapel's Sunday School Anniversary, children from the other Chapel would, so it is said, kill snails to make sure it rained the next day. This would spoil the parade through the village to the Chapel, complete with its banners, band, BB and GLB in uniform, as well as all the Sunday School scholars and teachers. I only remember warm sunny days for Anniversary – the snail killing curse rarely worked!

I played in piano duets, 'The Witches' Flight' and the Overture to *Tancredi*, as part of the entertainment at Mount Zion Chapel Christian Endeavour Concerts. Down Chapel had Wesley Guild and there was a Junior Guild, led by Mr. Jukes, as well. We had our first opportunity to speak publicly at these meetings. We prepared papers researching material on famous Christians. Guild was a great training ground for many people.

After many requests, the GLB obtained permission from the St. Clement's Chapel Trustees to learn country dancing in the Sunday School Hall. The Chapel leaders frowned upon any form of dancing in those days!

*1st Penzance Company of the GLB*
*(l. to r.) Back row:Joan Ladner, Kathleen Hall, Beryl Williams, Dorothy Hosking,*
*Estelle Hosking, Lily Polgrean, Audrey Eddy, Thelma Eddy, Dora Price (with flag)*
*Middle row: Ruth Pomeroy, Edith Harvey, Path Jeffrey, Capt. Janie Pender, Jean*
*Wallis, Maureen Richards, Kathleen Johns*
*Front row: Ann Quick, Mary Llewellyn, Margaret Johns, Margaret Harvey, Carol*
*Biddle, Jacqueline Wallis, Pamela Hocking*

When a Liberal candidate for Parliament was canvassing for votes in our area his sister, June Allison, came along to help him. She started a club for young Liberals in the Salvation Army building in Commercial Road. It was a youth club and many of us joined. We took part in quizzes and listened to talks. We were not concerned with the politics then. This small club closed when the leader left the village.

John Grose became my special boyfriend. Although born in Mousehole, he spent many of the pre-war years wherever his father, who was in the Royal Navy, was stationed. He came to Mousehole with his mother and brother to stay with Grandma Harvey in Commercial Road. He transferred from Plymouth College to Penzance Boys' County School when the heavy bombing started in Plymouth. He then transferred to Devonport High School for Boys when they were evacuated to Penzance. He went back to Plymouth when Devonport High School returned after the war. We corresponded and he came back to stay at Grandma Harvey's for his holidays. John's family attended Mount Zion Chapel and lived near the Chapel.

It has been said that the large blue elvan rock outside Mount Zion Chapel was on the line of division between the blue elvan and granite on which the village was built. The part of the village north of the river and the rocks on the Newlyn side were of blue elvan, and the southern part and the rocks to the Cave and beyond were of granite.

Paul Feast at the beginning of October was observed by all the Mousehole folk as well as the inhabitants of Paul and Sheffield. There were stalls on the Green which was just across the road from Paul Church. There was food and drinks as well as more wonderful 'wacko', the round spirals of cream and burnt sienna coloured toffee. Mousehole Male Voice Choir gave a Concert at Paul Church for the Feast Celebrations and many of the older boys had joined the Choir. So the girls could study the men fully at this time and they were an appreciative audience of the music.

Paul Church suffered some bomb damage from a 'near miss', our most serious air raid. I heard the bombs explode from our Morrison table shelter in our kitchen. The Island was the only casualty at Mousehole. It was machine gunned or bombed. In the darkness it was probably mistaken for a large ship. We could sometimes see the sky redden over the low hills across the bay and knew that the Falmouth area was being attacked by enemy raids. The ships and docks there were the target. We were glad that we were not having constant raids and felt sorry for the stress caused in those who were.

When the war was over, I spent a holiday in Pudsey, near Leeds, with Auntie Gladys and Uncle Luther. Auntie Rene stayed with us for part of the holiday and we travelled to Leeds and Bradford and other places by bus. The cities were very smoky and the buildings grubby in those days. I know that my new red jacket had finger marks on the shoulder after standing next to a workman on a packed bus.

Auntie Gladys and Uncle Luther took me to the Alhambra Theatre in Bradford to see the D'Oyley Carte Opera company performing "Iolanthe". This was a wonderful evening and I was enthralled by the singing and acting. I even remember Uncle Luther bringing us coffee in the interval and I watched the well-dressed audience as I drank the coffee.

A few older fishermen acted as 'Guides to the Cave'. They asked visitors to let them show them the way to the Cave and tell them tales of smugglers. Of course, they expected a fee for this service!

In my teens I visited the Cave rocks frequently and explored the area. On one occasion I climbed over the large rocks as far as Penzer Point to return using the pathway below the Watch House. I remember that, on the way, I had to jump over a deep wide gully. I did this with John's help and encouragement, but I never repeated this expedition. It was important to know the state of the tides for such explorations, and I would not recommend anyone without knowledge of the tides or without a reasonable degree of agility to attempt this scramble. It was, admittedly, further than the visit made by the 'Guides'!

One evening I was walking homewards through Mousehole village, after spending the evening with a friend who lived at the opposite end of the village from where I lived. Suddenly, as the sky darkened, the sky turned red. As the glow deepened and flickered villagers came out from their homes and gathered together in groups.

*The Cave entrance*

They pointed to the sky as they began to get distressed; they said they had never seen anything like it. I stopped walking and stood by the harbour listening to the babble. It was the end of the world arriving, they declared. Some cried, others prayed and the rest ran into their houses. "The sky is on fire", was the crowd's decision. I stood with the remaining group and then a knowledgeable man informed us we were watching the Aurora Borealis, known as the Northern Lights, glowing in the sky and there was nothing to fear.

I hurried home. Indoors, my parents had not noticed anything extraordinary. Of course, nothing serious happened, but there was certainly some hysterical fear in the village that evening.

Another memorable event was the crash of a small yellow aircraft, an autogiro, at the top of the hill. It crashed just inside the gateway leading to the field by the side of the collapsed roof of Mousehole Cave. This was an unexpected happening which provided the villagers with an outing to go and view it, and talk about it. It was another site for souvenir hunters to add pieces to their collections. Most of the village boys had a piece of the wreckage. This was not as exciting to me as the Aurora Borealis. Most of the girls were just pleased that the pilot was not badly injured.

*My Bicycle*

Grandpa Polgrean and my father, Arnold Polgrean, had been organists at Mount Zion Chapel. Perhaps this was the reason that made Auntie Phyllis promise me a bicycle if I played the organ at Mount Zion for a Service. Perhaps she thought that once I played the organ I would become 'hooked' and continue playing.

My music teacher, Maybelle Cotton, gave me some lessons on the organ and I learned about pedals and stops. I was interested in the different sounds obtained by pulling out various stops but was not impressed by using the pedals with my feet. However, I did want a bicycle.

The organ had no electricity and a hand pump had to be used to make it play. This was known as 'blowing' and was done by pushing a lever up and down behind the organ. My mother did this for me to practise on the organ. Jimmy Virgo was the official 'blower'.

It was arranged that I should practise on the organ and when I could play chosen hymns well, I should play for a Service. I believe this was a weeknight Service and of course Auntie Phyllis attended. But I did not play the organ in church again after this service.

Afterwards I received my £5 for my bicycle. My life was enhanced by this present. I could go on bike rides with friends and to otherwise inaccessible coves for picnics. I learned to ride the bike by going along Top Lane, from Raginnis to the Ring and Thimble. When proficient enough I did this ride and then continued to Newlyn and down Paul Hill (a test for the brakes!), through the Newlyn Fishmarket area and back home to Mousehole. It was a testing 'push' up Newlyn Slip and Raginnis Hill.

*Learning to ride at Top Lane*

All this was done without a bicycle bell. One day as I was going through Newlyn I almost did a Belgian fisherman a mischief when he walked in front of my bike. I braked and just avoided catching him between his legs. Luckily he was not facing towards me. I could not understand his Belgian language and escaped from him with a rueful smile and a 'Sorry!' in English.

Auntie Phyllis heard of my 'accident' and brought along a bicycle bell to Miss Wesley's School. She was not allowed to call me out of my lesson but the receptionist smilingly gave me the bell after lessons. Dear eccentric Auntie Phyllis had wrapped up the bell in a square of felt and secured the felt with large safety pins!

*Mousehole Harbour, 1930s*

# More Aspects of Village Life

*Shopping*

Miss Eddy's shop was at the bottom of steep Raginnis Hill and was a food/chemist/sweet shop. She sold most articles that one would need. The bread was crusty and the cakes tasted home-made. The cream was yellow with a thick crusty topping. There were fruit and vegetables on wooden slatted shelves near the door. Nail files, scissors, hair nets and shampoos were secured by elastic bands to hanging cardboard holders fixed to the wall. The eucalyptus oil board hung next to the Vaseline and baby powder, and on the shelf next to them was my favourite shampoo - coconut oil. The perfumes mingled, but did not conflict. Errands to the shop were a pleasure; there were no crowds or long queues or trolleys to push. Purchases were wrapped in tissue paper or stacked neatly in brown paper bags. The goods were then stowed away in our cane shopping baskets. We were very proud of our coloured woven baskets. I had one which was a very acceptable birthday present.

There were butchers' shops delivering fresh meat to the customer's requirements. Pasty meat was 'skirt', not minced beef. One of the butcher's shops was near the school and so was Pasterella's sweet shop. The sweets I remembered were liquorice bootlaces and sticks, which were affordable from our pocket money. We also liked coconut cushions, violet cashews, aniseed balls, sherbet and pear drops. Sweethearts had loving messages written in icing sugar across them. There were penny chocolate bars and cherry drops.

Herbert Victor sold his watercolour paintings from his front window. 'Dickna' (Richard) Ladner had a newsagents on the 'Cliff' overlooking the harbour. The back room was a men's hairdressers and many children also had their haircuts there.

At one time there were two fish and chip shops: Billy and Eileen Harvey owned the one nearer to us and I was sent on the errand of getting supper there many times. There was a little haberdashery in the front room of a house near the Millpool. I bought cottons, needles and elastic from Lilian who ran the well-stocked shop. There was a shoe store, several grocers, a cobbler, where I went with the family shoes to be mended, and the Post Office on the corner where the road came onto the harbour front. The Postmaster, Bill Blewett, achieved fame by acting character parts (himself!) in several films, so his wife had the main responsibility of running the post office.

Mr. Pentreath ran the Stores, which was a depot for coal and paraffin. My mother sent me there for paraffin for our oil heaters. The can, when filled, was very heavy and I remember it seemed to drag my shoulder down to my knees when I carried it back up Raginnis Hill.

Joe Rowe had a bake house in the alley at the back of the 'Ship' Inn. I took to him saffron cakes and Christmas cakes made by my mother and Joe shovelled them into the big hot oven. They were left to cook and I fetched them later when they were ready. A small payment was made for the cooking. I remember that some of the Christmas cakes were at times highly coloured but not burnt. Many of my friends' mothers took the weekend joint or whole meals along to be cooked.

There was one pub, the well-known 'Ship' Inn on the harbour front and I was sent to the back door for soda water when my brother was sick. Legend has it that in a period of severe storms and bad weather, the village was starving. A fisherman, Tom Bawcock, put to sea and caught seven sorts of fish in a miraculous catch which saved the village. The 'Ship' commemorates this on Tom Bawcock's Eve (23rd December) by cooking 'Starry-gazey Pie' with seven sorts of fish.

There was a Chemist's shop on the Bank opposite the Post Office and this was later replaced by a drug store which also sold ice cream. In Chapel Street, Warren's had a shop selling confectionery, where we ordered our pasties. Then there was a restaurant above the shop.

We went to the Penzance shops for clothing and luxury goods, including more expensive underwear and foundation garments. Best shoes also came from Penzance, as we had to make the most of our clothing coupons. Cosmetics were in short supply during the war years. At sixteen, I had my first lipstick, which was in a cardboard container and felt as dry as a crayon. My first perfume was 'Californian Poppy' in a tiny bottle, but my favourites were 'Gardenia', even though it was in a small plain bottle, and 'Evening in Paris', which was very up-market to us in those years.

We borrowed books from the Free Library at the top of Morrab Road, although Mr. Ladner, the newsagent, had a small 'pay' stock of books for the romantics for the cost of a few pence per week.

The larger grocery stores in Penzance had agents who would visit houses in the village weekly, taking orders for basic cooking ingredients and any delicacies they could persuade the housewives to buy. It was always a delight for the younger children to await the arrival of the box from Penzance and to examine the contents.

Shopping in Penzance was as exciting as anywhere at this time. There were drapery department stores, bookshops and large shops selling chinaware and gifts. Mother and I could eat out in fish and chip shops; in small cafés we could lunch on pasties with a cup of tea. After our lunch, we visited a sweet shop and I usually chose coconut mushrooms. We ate our sweets in the Savoy Cinema, Causewayhead and enjoyed a few hours of escapism watching romantic films. Elderly people who lived in Mousehole rarely travelled further than Penzance.

*Transport*

When my mother went to Penzance to work at the West End Drapery Stores, she went by wagonnette. When I needed transport to Penzance to attend Miss Wesley's Commercial College and then to work as a secretary, I was lucky to have the choice of two bus services. The Western National supplied season tickets for the journey. The other buses (local) provided transport for cash. There was a Western National service running every half hour, at a quarter to and quarter past the hour. The local buses, 'Necky' (Nicholas) Harvey and his two sons, Vincent and Pomeroy, and the Hitchens ran their buses on the hour and half hour. Many local people were loyal to the local buses and would only travel with them.

From Mousehole I caught the bus on the Cliff when it turned by the village clock or I went up to the terminus on the Parade. The Penzance terminus was in draughty Albert Street by the Station with various pick-up points on the way, including the Greenmarket and the Promenade at the bottom of Alexandra Road. I used the Western National bus because I had a season ticket, but most locals would catch the locally owned buses. They would stop anywhere for you and fill to overflowing. 'Necky' Harvey was renowned for 'always having room for one more'. I remember the occasion when Estelle and I and friends were on our way in her car to play tennis on the Promenade courts in Newlyn when she had a puncture by the weighbridge just before we reached Newlyn. As it happened, the Hitchens bus, driven by Billy Treleven, was passing at the time. He stopped, seeing our predicament, got out of the bus, and sorted out our problem before continuing on his route. His passengers accepted it as part of their journey. I cannot imagine this happening nowadays.

During the summer months I rode my bicycle to work. I had a deep wicker basket on the front of my bicycle and I carried my books in this.

Ordinary traffic was limited because of the petrol rationing at this time. There was time to dream and breathe in the fresh salt breezes as I went along the seaside road. In fact, all the travel was enjoyable.

*The Yglesias sisters*

I remember Dorothy Yglesias when she lived in Cherry Orchard, the house just above the row of houses which Grandpa Eddy owned when I was young. Dorothy had her pet jackdaw and had begun the wild bird sanctuary in her garden. The garden also had lovely sweet pea and other flowers and I went to her each year for my posy of flowers which I carried when we walked in procession behind our St. Clement's Wesleyan Banners on Anniversary Sunday. (This was in my childhood, before I marched in procession with the Girl's Life Brigade in my teens.)

I remember Dorothy's little round crochet hats which she always wore. Phyllis, known as 'Pog', had fuzzy dark hair and wore trousers and an artist's smock. Both sisters were kind and were of Spanish descent. They involved themselves in caring for wild birds, especially those injured. The sisters built cages and runs, taking up more space in the garden as their work grew.

Dorothy especially was a good friend to my mother, who greatly appreciated the flowering plant Dorothy brought to her every Christmas. I went up the hill and their garden steps frequently to see the wild birds and to watch Dorothy or Pog feed them. The birds grew to trust them completely and their 'pet' birds were allowed free range of their house.

# My First Job

My first job was Secretary to a Chartered Land Agent, Major Gilbert Evans, who was recently a central character in a book called 'Summer in February' by Jonathon Smith. If you have read the book you will know that it was about the Newlyn artists when Major Evans acted as Agent for Colonel Paynter's Estate and when the Major was based at Lamorna.

Our office was in Penzance. I began my work when the ground floor of a house became his new office and Major Evans took over the management of several more Estates.

At that time, the Major had married and had two boys. I knew nothing about his former days as friend to the Lamorna artists until I read the book about his earlier life.

The Principal of the private Commercial College where I had studied obtained jobs for her students, so I just walked in, so to speak.

Our office had gas lights and a gas fire. This seemed to be sufficient for our needs and it was many months before we went on to electric power. There was no telephone either, and I remember the excitement when the black instrument finally came and connected us to the world, reducing my typing duties. My typewriter was an old black 'sit up and beg' model, and my chair a hard 'kitchen-type' model. However, I faced the window and it was a large one, allowing me to see passers-by and whoever would be walking up the path to ring the doorbell. I had another desk with a lift-up sloping lid and another hard chair to sit on when I worked on the ledgers, from cashbook to final balance sheet, for each Estate. There was a grey steel filing cabinet and one bookcase. Major Evans had a lovely mahogany desk and a desk chair with padded seat and arms situated in the same room.

Estate duties took him out of the office, so I was frequently alone, and I remember being quite frightened the winter I sat in just gas lighting. What a difference a bright electric light makes. I always placed a saucer of water in front of our gas fire as I had been told that gas took all the moisture from the air, and fumes could be dangerous. One of my duties was tracing in Indian ink with a steel pen from maps of the various Estates, and I enjoyed this. Of course, all entries in the ledgers were handwritten by me with my fountain pen.

I travelled to the office by bus, or I cycled the three miles each way during the summer months. The only leave of absence I remember was for two days during the winter of 1947 when even Cornwall had heavy snowfalls preventing any movement of traffic. For two days I tobogganed on tea trays down the village hills with friends. On the third day of the freeze I walked the three miles to the office. And I walked back home again in the afternoon.

Holidays taken were two weeks in the summer and Bank Holidays including Christmas Day and Boxing Day. I was happy with my situation.

We held wonderful Rent Courts quarterly, when the farmers and house tenants paid their rentals and reported repairs which should be attended to. The notables (the gentry, as we would say) calling, Colonels, Judges, the Major's housekeeper as well as the tenants. I became very fond of the elderly folk. There was petrol rationing and coupons for everything, but I had pleasure in the little things of life. It was wonderful working for an employer who was gentlemanly and who always treated me with respect and these were matters taken for granted.

A highlight of my working life was when His Honour, the Lord of the Manor's son, came of age. All the tenant farmers, the Major and his wife and myself were invited. I had been seated opposite a young Naval officer cadet and my favourite lady tenants were around me. It was a light-hearted occasion with good food and conversation. I had promised to meet my boyfriend in the town nearby, after this lunch. I found I was the first to leave the Manor and felt very embarrassed, especially when His Honour told me that country dancing and the Sir Roger de Coverley were to follow. Obviously, I had been expected to join in with the dancing. Then some of the older tenants begged to leave, and I felt relieved. (I was not reprimanded by the Major, and he and his wife came to my wedding and reception.)

When I left the office to go to the North of England where my husband had obtained a teaching position, the Major said how very sorry he was I was leaving. I trained another girl to take my place and the Major gave me a glowing reference, which I still have, now over fifty years later.

# Courtship

John went back to Plymouth with his mother and brother David who was ten years younger than him. His father was serving on HMS *Bonaventure* in Mediterranean waters escorting convoys to Malta and taking part in the battle for Crete. He was killed when the ship was torpedoed by an Italian submarine. The family was at Mousehole with Grandma Harvey. This had been a very sad time for them in 1941 when John was thirteen years old and before we had met. In fact, I had not even noticed him at this time. He attended Mount Zion, 'Up' Chapel with his family and I attended 'Down' Chapel, the Wesleyans.

*John's father*

Like most of my friends, I had crushes on some of the boys in our Chapel circle and on boys I met briefly at friends' and neighbours' houses. I remember there was a handsome Naval cadet staying in 'Rosedene' during the time Grandma Eddy had let the house to a family. I had been invited several times to make up a 'four' for games, but I was young at the time and was regarded as a child to be tolerated as a playmate!

So, from the age of fifteen or sixteen, we were part of the crowd who enjoyed meeting at joint Chapel 'get-togethers' at each other's churches. John was a member of the Boys' Brigade and I was in the Girls' Life Brigade. We invited our opposite members to our parties, concert practices, play readings and outings.

As time passed we 'paired off' and went on cycle rides, walks and to concerts, plays and special activities. We played tennis together and enjoyed matches with friends on the Newlyn tennis courts in the seafront gardens near Newlyn Art Gallery.

Compared to today's romances I suppose our courtship would be considered very innocent and low key, but we bonded together and quietly enjoyed each other's company.

When I was seventeen, John returned to Plymouth and we corresponded regularly. This correspondence included my French exercises as I had decided to learn the language, and John was taking the subject in his Advanced School Certificate.

John and I missed each other's company and we were joyfully reunited when he came back to Mousehole for the school holidays.

*Photo taken from the Island*

We borrowed a punt from a relative and John sculled out of the harbour to St. Clement's Island. When we touched the rocks, John went on to the island to explore. When he returned to the punt, he suggested that I might like to see the island, too. It was a first for me, so, overcoming my fear and taking the box camera with me, I jumped over the clear deep water.

I took the photo of John in the boat and then explored the island. I was not impressed by the sharp rocks with just a few tufts of springy turf and, of course, the seagull droppings all around me. The rock had many barnacles attached to it. There was a hump in the middle part with a large rock, the Halse stone, and a cube of rock (the Bolitho Stone) was cemented on top of this. This was known to us all as the 'Pepperpot'. Many people have swum from the Cove to the Island and back again. They must have been brave to do this and had more 'puff' than I have. I was glad to get back to the boat and then to return to the safety of the harbour. It was not really a romantic trip. I would not like to have had a picnic there as many local families did in the past.

We enjoyed going on the many lovely walks around Mousehole.

Old Hill was one such walk, very steep if attacked from the bottom at the back of the Wesleyan Chapel, and quite rugged and narrow. Wild flowers, according to the season, flourished in the hedgerows and we enjoyed identifying them. I picked and pressed them, and this became a lifelong hobby. This hill led to Love Lane, a pretty level walk with views of Mousehole and the Wild Birds' Hospital.

Then, there was the walk to Lamorna and back again. I usually went via the Crackers and on through the Kemyels, coming back via Castallack, Top

Lane and the Ring and Thimble. The walk by Cave Lane led to the picnic spot known as the Battery and on to the large seaside boulders. Here we had views of the Bible Rock, which looked like a large open book. Just offshore was the Merlin Rock, easily accessible at low tide. Legend has it that this was where the Spanish

*Choir Outing to Padstow*

landed when they invaded Mousehole in 1595. I did not scramble over these rocks but John had done so. To me these rocks were dangerous: the water was very deep here and the rocks could be surrounded by heavy waves.

On the Newlyn side of the village, the beaches, the first cove, the boys' cove and the girls' cove were more to my liking and I enjoyed scrambling over them, examining various seaweeds and shells on the way. 'Sandy', which was reached at low tide from the boys' cove, was an interesting scramble. The rocks were covered in slippery, wonderful examples of seaweed and needed careful footwork. Sandy was a gully of clear water between the low water rocks and a fairly large rock. There was a patch of sand under the water, hence its name. The gap to swim was 7 or 8 yards wide. It was possible to walk across at extremely low spring tides, but it was a swimming place at times of the usual low tide. We all knew that there was a deep pit at the bottom of the large rock and avoided this spot, which was always filled with bootlace seaweed.

Another longer jump over a deep chasm and water was taken when John and I scrambled over the rocks from the Battery and the Cave towards the rocks beneath the Coastguard lookout at the end of the Crackers. I was not very athletic, but there was no way back to the Cave as the tide was coming in. I have never enjoyed walking on a landing stage to get to a boat (not even in Venice!)

Another walk John and I liked was to the Crackers and then to continue past the Coastguard lookout along the rough track which went to Lamorna by way of the cliffs; an occasional rock scramble was needed where paths petered out. We went past the rocks sloping gently into the sea known as 'Slinky Dene' and then around the magnificent granite headland of Carn Dhu guarding the entrance to Lamorna Cove. It was a lovely walk in Springtime when the daffodils were in bloom. This is now a popular section of the Cornwall Coastal Footpath, but it was rarely used in our day. At Lamorna we often took the cliff path, which started just beyond the quay. This became difficult to follow after a short distance, but led to secluded coves and cliffs before reaching the Logan Rock and Porthcurno, but we never attempted to go that far. This was the real 'wreckers coast' of times past and was so dangerous that a remote-controlled lighthouse was installed at Tater Dhu in recent years.

At the top of Raginnis Hill, just below the beginning of the path to Love Lane was an old granite seat which was built into the hedge of Love Lane. It was a good viewing point over the village and a good resting spot for the elderly after climbing the Hill or a stopping place for young people to sit and have a cuddle. This seat formed one of my Mousehole memories.

A favourite group walk with young people from both Chapels took place after the Sunday evening service. John and I joined in this walk to Penzance Promenade where many groups of young people from the area would walk to and fro. We would walk back to Mousehole and would usually stop for an enjoyable cup of coffee on the way at the café at the top of Newlyn Slip.

The cinema was popular, enabling us to live in someone else's world – the more glamorous the better! The back seats in the 'Gaiety' at Newlyn were a favourite of courting couples.

Our cycle rides took us to the Logan Rock and Porthcurno. Sometimes we would go to Land's End. We cycled to Penzance, Marazion and on to Prussia Cove, where we saw the wreck of the old battleship *Warspite* just after it had been the scene of a daring rescue by the Mousehole     (Penlee) lifeboat. I was initiated into the rules of Rugby and we often went to the Mennaye Field to see the 'Pirates' (Penzance and Newlyn).

*The 'Warspite' at Prussia Cove*

*View from Raginnis Hill of the NATO Grand Fleet anchored in Mounts Bay, 1948*

*Telegraph Hill, London*
*Just engaged!*

John and I visited each other's houses for teas or suppers when he was on holiday and I sometimes went to Plymouth and stayed with John, his mother, Ada Grose, and his brother David. We decided we wanted to marry and became engaged in 1948. John had left Devonport High School in 1946 and was studying French and Latin at Exeter University. He was exempt from National Service until he completed his post-graduate teaching year.

My work as a secretary for a Chartered Land Agent, was a 'reserved' occupation, which meant that I would not be called up for war work by joining the Armed Forces or Land Army. The work I was doing was considered equally important. In any case, compulsory service was lifted before I was eligible for call-up.

Maybell Cotton, my music teacher, arranged for me to stay for a weekend in Exeter with her relatives so that I could go to the University Ball with John. I was loaned a beautiful blue evening gown and we had a wonderful evening.

When I was twenty years old, John and I had a holiday together in London. It was the first time I had returned to London since my early childhood. We stayed in Sussex Gardens near Paddington Station. At that time, just after the war, this was where everyone from Cornwall stayed when they went to London. Of course, we had separate rooms. In those days we would not have contemplated anything else! My room had a wash-basin and hot water, but the toilet was along the corridor.

We bought our engagement rings at Bravingtons in the Strand. My ring was very pretty with three diamonds set in platinum. I bought John a gold signet ring. To celebrate our engagement we had tea in the nearby Lyons Corner House. The waitresses ('nippies') wore black dresses, white aprons and a white pleated headdress. It all seemed very posh to us in those days. We visited relatives of John's at Theydon Bois, at the end of the Tube in Essex, and proudly showed off our rings.

# Marriage

We decided to get married when John finished his studies. He wanted to join the Air Force and train as a pilot, but when he attended his medical he was graded 3 as it was found he had a perforated eardrum. He then had to start applying for teaching posts.

*Reception at St John's Hall, Penzance*

We were married on 15th July 1950 at St. Clement's Methodist Church. It was St. Swithun's Day and it rained and rained, but this did not spoil the happy occasion. John's cousin, Percy Harvey, was Best Man and my bridesmaids were Ruth Harvey and Margaret Harvey, cousins, and the Flower Girl was Kathleen Trevaskis. They wore aquamarine dresses, trimmed with lace and wore gold leaf headdresses. Derek, my brother, was an usher. He had left Penzance County School and joined the Naval School, HMS *St. Vincent*, so he wore his uniform.

I had decorated the church with pink rambling roses and carried a bouquet of pink roses with ferns. I had a long white dress and a headdress of white roses and orange blossom to hold my long veil in place. The dress had a

*Cutting the Cake*

printed pattern of lover's knots. My mother and I had travelled to Plymouth to buy the wedding outfit.

The guests and village people who thronged the Chapel for the wedding clasped their umbrellas and, remembering the recent Carnival when I was the bride in the tableau of 'The Bride wore boots', they told me that I would need my boots today! We did need an outsize umbrella to shelter us as we ran to the taxi which was taking us to our reception. The rain stopped as we boarded the train at Penzance Station.

Our reception was held at St. John's Hall, Penzance and Chirgwins made the cake and did the catering for us and for all our families and friends. Aunt Flo, Grandpa's youngest sister, and her family sent the ingredients for the cake from Canada and the cake was wonderful. Although there was still rationing, we had a lovely reception.

Aunt Flo's son, cousin Sid Haines, had visited us at Mousehole during the war while he was serving in the Canadian Army. He had taken me to the cinema in Penzance and held my hand during the film 'Gone with the Wind'. During his visit he met Ivris Chinn from Sheffield near Paul. Ivris worked in the Wool Shop in Causewayhead, Penzance and had courted her. They married and she went to Canada with him. Grandma Eddy kept in touch with all our overseas relations by corresponding regularly.

We left for Exeter after our wedding and stayed overnight in a hotel. I wore my going-away outfit for the train journey from Penzance – it was a powder blue suit, white blouse, black shoes, black gloves, and I carried a black handbag. My nylons had a seam at the back - high fashion - and Aunt Flo had sent them to me in a Canadian parcel. I felt very elegantly dressed. The next day we travelled on to London and went to Auntie Rene's flat in Hackney. Auntie Rene came to our wedding and was staying on in Mousehole for her holiday, leaving us to enjoy her flat in her absence.

On our honeymoon, we spent most days exploring the usual London tourist spots. We went to the theatre to see the current musicals ('Oklahama', 'Annie Get your Gun' and 'Hellzapoppin'), and plays where the atmosphere was magical. Of course, we did a little cooking, too, having romantic suppers at the flat.

I went back to the office on my return after a fortnight away to a mountain of work. There had been no 'temp' in my absence.

John was now applying in earnest for teaching posts. This was proving difficult at this late stage, since he should have started applying at Easter. To make things more difficult most posts were now being filled by ex-Service men who were older with more experience. He had several interviews and it was depressing being pipped at the post by these older men.

We were living at my Mother's and I happily continued my Sunday School and Girls' Life Brigade interests with other Church activities. I also enrolled with a Singer Sewing Course at Penzance, going to weekly lessons and using Grandma Eddy's sewing machine for my homework. (She gave me the machine later on.) I made a green button-through dress with long sleeves and cuffs. I learnt a lot of professional finishing touches and was proud of my efforts.

John made a superb Readicut moon shape rug, a proud possession for our future home. He also made a bookcase for my mother.

Eventually John obtained a temporary supply teaching post at St. Ives School, travelling there with Ken Johns, a teacher who also lived in Mousehole. The teacher he was replacing returned to work after a few weeks and John continued his applications. He went to York for an interview for a post teaching French at a private school in West Hartlepool in County Durham. There was an offer of a large unfurnished flat owned by the headmaster, Mr. Gallimore, for a rental of £2.50 a week, almost half the starting salary. John took the position, which was to start in January 1951.

John was a temporary postman for the Christmas period of 1950 and our first Christmas together was spent in Mousehole. I made my first Christmas cake, a great success. Cheese straws were my speciality and sponge cakes were successful, so with Mother's famous pudding, we had a great time. We held our party on Christmas evening and we spent the rest of the Christmas days visiting relatives. It was a happy time, but I was back in the office in Penzance again on 27ᵗʰ December and for the rest of the week, Saturday morning included, as usual. There were fond farewells and presents were given by my employers, including Major Evans, and Mr. W. Pezzack, for whom I did typing when the Major was on his regular visits to Wales.

The next week was spent packing up our possessions. Mother gave me her piano, which was going to West Hartlepool by carrier as soon as we were settled. We were sad to leave Mousehole and all our friends, but I had a gut feeling that, at some time in our lives, we would return to Cornwall again. Meanwhile, there would be holidays to look forward to. We left on Saturday 6th January for West Hartlepool via an overnight stop in London.

*Mousehole from The Rocks*

# Mousehole Dialect

I have tried to recall the dialect words and phrases which were in common use when I was growing up in the village.  Some are normal English words, but with quite different meanings; others are in general use in Cornwall and especially in West Penwith, but there are some which are peculiar to the village.  This may be due to the fact that, until the First World War, the village was virtually a closed community, with little outside contact apart from fishing.

| | |
|---|---|
| better fit | the wiser course would be |
| a fly-by-night | an empty-headed girl |
| clubbish | brutal |
| dung dabber | a child continually getting filthy |
| slones | sloes |
| whilk | a stye on the eye |
| pisky stool | toadstool or mushroom |
| gone round land | away from home longer than expected |
| morgy | dogfish (with rough scales) (rough as a morgy) |
| chaffin | very thirsty |
| gone abroad | dissolved |
| marinates | almost always the pilchards when marinated |
| munge | to chew, knead or squeeze |
| clunk | to swallow |
| skeeten down | heavy rainfall |
| meddlen | so and so (as regards health) |
| leary | hungry and tired |
| minchin | playing truant |
| 'ee d' come from Dava Downs | an uncouth, untidy person |
| soursops | sorrel leaves |
| like a bundle of straw tied in the middle | an untidy person, usually fat |
| cob | forelock, neatly combed above the forehead |

| | |
|---|---|
| shegeen | cuttlefish used between bars of bird cages |
| kywiggle | to manage, manoeuvre |
| huffy | a perk – a free drink or meal if working in a café |
| caboolen or plouncer | stone with a hole through it with a rope attached (used by fishermen to frighten fish to the opening of a seine net) |
| jowster | fish hawker |
| pulled through a gorse bush backwards | untidy appearance, especially hair |
| put a piece on someone | to excuse someone's failings |
| durns | doorframe, doorpost |
| leat | small stream |
| linhay (linnie) | open sided shelter at side of cottage |
| platt | small landing |
| ope or dran | narrow opening between houses |
| flasket | large wicker clothes basket |
| caggled | caked with dirt |
| caudle | mess, muddle |
| she's proper thurt | she's in an awkward mood |
| maazed | bewildered |
| brebm | very – he's brebm good to me |
| can 'ee mind? | do you remember? |
| sumper | a soaking (especially by a wave) |
| midgen | tiny amount |
| dreckly | later on, perhaps |
| three scats behind | very late or slow |
| strove me down | contradicted |
| brought to one pass | clothes worn without regard for 'best' wear |
| sharps | shafts of cart or wagon |
| spitten image | exactly alike |
| stagged with mud | caked with mud |
| click | to get off with a girl |

| | |
|---|---|
| stank | to tread heavily |
| stave | to make a lot of noise |
| grizzle | to grin, snigger |
| wacka | brown and cream peppermint (a coil of this sold at the Corpus Christi Fair) |
| stay your stomach | something to eat for the time being |
| scrowls | bits left when pork fat is melted down |
| grouchens | tealeaves left in cup or teapot |
| crease the tea | dilute tea with hot water |
| boughten | shop cake – not home made |
| crimp | join the dough edges of a pasty |
| tap | mend the sole of footwear – the sole itself |
| brandis | stand on which the kettle rested |
| canvas | floor covering, lino |
| shoat | outflow of a spring piped to the roadside |
| dressed to kill | overdressed |
| hard as Pharoah | obstinate |
| screechen like a whitneck | screaming like a weasel |
| mouth open like a chaw | someone anxious to eat (like a crow) |
| wisht as a winnard | as miserable as a redwing in the cold |
| pilf | filmy, feathery dust under the bed |
| flinked | flounced out in anger |
| lem (of the wicked) | limb of the devil – a mischievous boy |
| all shremmy | feeling a cold is developing |
| tifflings | loose ends of cotton from sewing |
| gook | bonnet (blue?) peaked in front like old nursery rhyme illustrations |

| | |
|---|---|
| cue | metal plate on footwear to prevent toe of sole from wearing thin |
| coming out like rope | complimentary term to a good speaker |
| mouth scat abroad | gaping with surprise |
| more tongue than teeth | chatterbox |
| big as bull's beef | big-headed, domineering |
| limp as a ling | weak |
| scad | horse mackerel |
| hollen like a thatcher | shouting loudly |
| laughing like a pisky | mischievously |
| like a cow handling a musket | very clumsy |
| sick as a shag | poorly |
| plum as ull | soft as wool, stupid |
| floshed | beaten or whipped (egg in milk) |
| rich | delicious |
| she's rich (to a child) | beautiful, lovely |
| all behind like a cow's tail | late |
| come in like a gale of wind | boisterous entry |
| the tea's like bark | very strong and dark (bark was the tanning liquid for fishing nets) |
| dip | 'eeny, meeny, miny, mo' – the first one out was 'dip' |
| ruckle | push along an iron hoop with a 'drill' |
| bread and cheese | hawthorn leaves (edible) |
| chibbles | small onions |
| cuddy | one's particular territory when blackberrying |
| policeman's buttons | blue scabious |
| hurts | whortleberries |
| stog | small log for the fire |
| cheens | small of back or kidney area |

83

| | |
|---|---|
| traade | rubbish |
| eavin | very dirty (of a house) |
| poaming | thrashing, hitting |
| skeeter | water syringe (usually brass) for cleaning windows |
| tut | a stool for raising the feet, pouffée |
| sheath | oven baking tray |
| flies | hands of a clock |
| riddle | rake out a fire |
| tie | bed mattress |
| fit | cook or make |
| jammy maw | slice of bread and jam |
| raw fry | any leftovers fried up in a pan |
| thunder and lightning | bread with golden syrup and clotted cream |
| scat'n 'ome | shut it tight |
| crease oil | creosote |
| piddly bed | dandelions |
| murfles | freckles |
| poshy | wheezy |
| laverack | boy always getting wet on the shore |
| nearly | miserly |
| miffed | offended |
| thurt-eyed | cross-eyed |
| wished | off-colour, miserable |
| chuck | choke |
| ratsmeat | cow parsley |
| spickety | speckled |
| bullhorn | a snail |
| zawn | deep cleft in the cliffs |
| oarweed | seaweed |
| ancient as the Mount | precocious child or a droll young person |
| train | oil pressed from pilchards |
| shales | fish scales |
| smeech | acrid smell |
| foochen (about) | poking around |
| plummery | bread set to rise |
| fitty | correctly done |

| | |
|---|---|
| asleep | mildew - 'the tablecloth's asleep' |
| spence | cupboard under the stairs |
| buzza | earthenware crock |
| clidge | to stick fast |
| stream | to rinse |
| riffles | slates missing after a storm |
| timnynoggy | odd, shapeless thing |
| codge-up | slovenly piece of work |
| meryans | ants |
| splits | bread buns |
| footy | April 1st (fooled 'ee?) |
| quiddles | spider crabs |
| cankers | harbour crabs |
| towser | coarse apron |
| 'Turk' | very naughty child (from Turkish and Barbary pirates of middle ages) |
| besoms | heather brooms |
| geek | peep, have a look at |
| scat | blow |
| piggal | heavy iron digger |
| niceys | sweets |
| muctions | rubbish |
| bod | fish in rockpool |
| bullcat | fish (smaller) in rockpool |
| cherks | half-consumed cinders |
| tubbin | piece of turf |
| teal | plant potatoes, etc |
| hailed up | pulled with great might and strength |
| carkers | toy cork boats |
| kiskeys | toy boats made from a reed |
| towrag | dried cod |
| dippy | white sauce |
| pasty | segment of an orange |
| peach | to entice |
| lagging | paddling barefoot |
| trannygoat | shag (cormorant) |
| zart | sea urchin |

# Changes in the Village
# (50 years later)

When I go to Mousehole now I notice that men no longer walk up and down the Cliff in their fishermen's clothes in quiet companionship with their friends. The old age pensioners' seat, which was once a meeting place for the older men and women of the village, is nowadays mainly used by holidaymakers with their young families. This is fine, but the whole character of the village is different.

Many houses have now become holiday homes, and are empty for much of the year. The small village grocery shops have disappeared or become art galleries and souvenir shops. There are more cafés, but there is still a fish and chip shop.

The Keigwin Arms, Mousehole's oldest house, dating from the days before the Spanish raid of 1595, a few years after the Armada, still remains.

The harbour is now used by yachts and pleasure boats instead of the family-owned fishing boats. Sand has been brought into the harbour and covers the sharp dark stones that I knew as a child. This is a great improvement for the children to enjoy. As you walk past the rocks on the northern side of the harbour, there is a man-made swimming pool for the children between the first and second coves where we used to swim.

St. Clement's Chapel still stands firm at the bottom of Raginnis Hill with memories of our marriage. There are other family links now - the war memorial tablet with the names of John's father and my cousin Harry. At the time of my brother's ordination into the Methodist Ministry, a brass altar cross with an inscription asking for prayers for his ministry was presented to the Church by my parents. Derek married a Mousehole girl, Kathleen Johns. There is also the remembrance corner for the crew of the lifeboat 'Solomon Browne'.

With diminishing numbers, Mount Zion Chapel closed and amalgamated with St. Clement's. The building was sold and has been converted into flats. The Girls' Life Brigade and the Boys' Brigade, the focus of much of our teenage years, no longer meet and both have been disbanded.

An addition to the village is a plaque on the front of a house in Parade Hill commemorating the fact that the house was the home of Joseph Trewavas.

Joseph had joined the Navy, and, as a result of an act of great bravery in the Crimean War, he became the first Naval VC in 1853. Joseph was John's mother's great-uncle and we were happy that we could attend the ceremony of the unveiling of this plaque with her. We also attended a function in Penzance when the VC was returned to Cornwall and displayed, with Joseph's other medals, in the Penlee House Museum.

I still have a warm feeling and a sense of calm enjoyment going through the village and think of the families who used to live in the houses I pass. The village and the narrow, winding streets are still the same as when I went to school there. But on the outskirts there are more houses, many with enlarged gardens.

*Joseph Trewavas, VC*

*The 'Solomon Browne' on the slip with passengers for Lifeboat Day*

The lifeboat is now based in Newlyn, but the old lifeboat house is still in its original position on Penlee Point and is kept as a memorial to the *Solomon Browne* and its crew.

The open river, which ran through the village when I was a child, has been covered over and a modern sewage system installed in the harbour.

Penlee Quarry, between Mousehole and Newlyn, is being converted into a marina. There is no longer the twice-daily stone blasting causing traffic to stop for several minutes at blasting times.

The tradition of the Christmas lights, which started while we were away from Cornwall, has continued, and every year more lights appear around the harbour and surrounding area. Floating set pieces brighten the harbour and pieces glow from the quays and hillside. Crowds of people visit the village every year. Many folk visit the Ship Inn restaurant on Tom Bawcock's Eve, December 23rd, to taste the famous starry-gazey pie now associated with the legend of the Mousehole Cat. The lights are switched on in a delightful ceremony with Mousehole Male Voice Choir singing from the bank above the pensioners' chairs in an outdoor concert. On December 19th, the lights are switched off for an hour to remember the lifeboat disaster.

I love the nostalgia of Mousehole and enjoy meeting and talking about my memories with old schoolfriends. The village is still a wonderful venue for artists and I have painted many scenes myself.

I am very happy to have had the opportunity to return to Cornwall, where I have lived for nearly fifty years at Falmouth.